Abeer Y. Hoque is a Nigerian born Bangladeshi American writer and photographer. She has published a book of travel photographs and poems called *The Long Way Home* (Ogro Dhaka 2013), and a book of linked stories, photographs and poems called *The Lovers and the Leavers* (Bengal Lights Books 2014, HarperCollins *Publishers* India 2015). She is a Fulbright Scholar and has received several other fellowships and grants. Her writing and photography have been published in *Guernica*, *Outlook Traveller*, *Wasafiri*, *ZYZZYVA*, *India Today*, and *The Daily Star*. She has degrees from the University of Pennsylvania's Wharton School of Business and an MFA in writing from the University of San Francisco.

For more information, visit olivewitch.com

ADVANCE PRAISE FOR *OLIVE WITCH*

… an intelligent, riveting, startlingly honest voice. The writing is elegant and remains exhilarating even when the events are dark.
– Chika Unigwe, author of *On Black Sisters Street*

It is not just the sweeping breadth of [Hoque's] life story, but the keen eye and insight she brings to her reminiscences, that make this an unusually affecting account. From the red dust of Nigeria to the grey pavement of urban America to the lush green of the Bangladeshi countryside, Hoque makes her worlds come alive in evocative, arresting language. Not since Michael Ondaatje have I read a writer who so seamlessly marries poetry with prose in their writing with such a deft, bittersweet touch.
– Zafar Sobhan, editor, *Dhaka Tribune*

Full of visceral landscapes, characters, and scenes from a life lived on three continents, *Olive Witch* is an intense examination of displacement and fragmentation, loss and getting over it. Written with honesty, intelligence, and an eye for sensual detail, this is a fierce and gorgeous memoir.
– Stephen Beachy, author of *Boneyard*

Sometimes as a reader you thirst for a tale that you don't know you are missing: *Olive Witch* is one of those. Hoque's book sings the migrant's tale in lush and heartbreakingly poetic prose … A brave and gorgeous new voice has arrived among us and I am thrilled to welcome her into the fold.
– Nayomi Munaweera, author of *Island of a Thousand Mirrors*

… vividly conveys each setting with its unique joys and heartaches and the complex parts they play in an ever-changing sense of self and home. The father-daughter relationship portrayed here is moving as well in its evolution over the decades.
– Pavani Yalamanchili, editor, *The Aerogram*

Boy, this is elegant writing: smooth, clean, sharp, but, with just enough wiggle. The writing is wonderfully alive, and drawn with such economy it gives the (false) impression of being easy. It's not. Abeer Hoque's natural lyricism is sustained by being contained and framed. She rolls but she controls, and she does it so well.
– Aaron Shurin, author of *The Skin of Meaning*

Some gorgeous writing. Spontaneous. Fresh. Fire in the belly fresh.
– Andrew Pham, author of *The Eaves of Heaven*

… a memoir that sneaks up on you, and suddenly you are captivated. Here is a story of finding one's place in a world that insists too strongly on national borders and other lines of division. Here is a story of crossing borders – of rising above burdens of identity, of learning to accept oneself as well as the circumstances of one's birth. Here is a story of one woman's journey to self-actualization.
– Chinelo Okparanta, author of *Under the Udala Trees*

An unflinching yet luminously beautiful take on family, race, sex and the treachery of memory. Don't be fooled by frangipani beauty of Abeer Hoque's prose. Its razor-sharp edges can draw blood.
– Sandip Roy, author of *Don't Let Him Know*

… traverses a wide emotional landscape, juxtaposing perceptions, moods, and events which though they seem disparate, form a compellingly authentic mirror for the fractured world we all share.
– Paul S. Flores, Susan Griffin, and Andrew Leland, judges for the Tanenbaum Award in Nonfiction from the San Francisco Foundation

PRAISE FOR *THE LOVERS AND THE LEAVERS*

… a multimedia, multi-genre experience … an ambitious undertaking, spirited and subtle. Yet for all of Hoque's impressive artistry, she seeks very recognizable ends: to give us a vivid sense of place as rich as the people who inhabit it and to render the inner lives of those people, to let us feel their passions and their pains – those that mark them and make them sometimes beautiful, sometimes broken, but always always compelling.
– Eric LeMay, New Books Network

Hoque captures a kind of simultaneous global existence beautifully.
– Scott Pinkmountain, The Make/Work podcast on *The Rumpus*

This lovingly produced book contains not just stories, it interleaves photographs with text, and the prose is broken by jagged lines of verse. Taken together, it produces an effect of a blinding swirl, of love glimpsed – but never quite found – through the eddies of time… Hoque's language can make you see anew.
– Amrita Dutta, *The Indian Express*

… a fine example of stylish storytelling.
– Jaya Bhattacharji Rose, publishing consultant and columnist, jayabhattacharjirose.com

The characters surface, lead you slowly to the edge, and you fall in love with them – and then they leave you for a moment, submerged on your own, reemerging in another story.
– Nadia Q. Ahmad, *Asian American Writers' Workshop*

Prose interleaves poetry interleaves photography. The effect is dazzling. The reader's pulse quickens in response to these remarkable stories in which eros is not examined so much as inhabited. Characters leave the pages of one story to resurface in another story at some other stage in life. They are lovers who leave, and they return as lovers.
– Mridula Koshy, author of *Not Only the Things That Have Happened*

Abeer Hoque gifts her readers three distinct pleasures in this collection of interconnected stories of intertwined lives and interwoven loves: the crystalline clarity of her photography, the quiet elegance of her poetry, and the vivid sensuality of her prose. Together, they bring to life modern Bangladesh and the lives and loves of its people, wherever they live.
– Salil Tripathi, author of *The Colonel Who Would Not Repent*

Hoque is one of the most exciting writers working both in and out of the sub-continent and her fiction is made up of that rare mixture: searingly clean passion alloyed with the courage to take risks with form.
– Ruchir Joshi, author of *The Last Jet-Engine Laugh*

Written with cool assurance, the interlinked stories … zing around our troubled and exciting globalized world.
– Kaiser Haq, author of *Pariah and Other Poems*

Lush and lyrical, raw and unnerving, *The Lovers and the Leavers* is an impressive debut; a sensuous, poignant exploration of the joys, complexities, and consequences of human desire and connectivity in a global age.
– Sheba Karim, author of *Skunk Girl*

Abeer Hoque's words sing from every page. In lyrical and playful prose, sometimes in the cadence of bansuri melodies, other times with the bounce of hard rock, these stories speak of love, fierce as a runaway car, soft as a moan. Sexy, cosmopolitan, and loaded with quiet humour.
– Mahmud Rahman, author of *Killing the Water*

Olive Witch

A MEMOIR

ABEER Y. HOQUE

First published in India in 2016 by Fourth Estate
An imprint of HarperCollins *Publishers* India

P-ISBN: 978-93-5177-700-7
E-ISBN: 978-93-5177-701-4

2 4 6 8 10 9 7 5 3 1

Abeer Y. Hoque asserts the moral right
to be identified as the author of this work.

The views and opinions expressed in this book are the author's own
and the facts are as reported by her, and the publishers are not in
any way liable for the same.

HarperCollins *Publishers*
A-75, Sector 57, Noida, Uttar Pradesh 201301, India
1 London Bridge Street, London, SE1 9GF, United Kingdom
Hazelton Lanes, 55 Avenue Road, Suite 2900, Toronto, Ontario M5R 3L2
and 1995 Markham Road, Scarborough, Ontario M1B 5M8, Canada
25 Ryde Road, Pymble, Sydney, NSW 2073, Australia
195 Broadway, New York, NY 10007, USA

Typeset in 11/14 Bembo by
R. Ajith Kumar

Printed and bound in the United States of America by
LSC Communications

To my parents for their gifts of adventure and honour
To Simi because she will always understand
And to Maher for his light and laugh

Contents

bow echo, 73°F

> I swallowed and melted into the tar-patched roof. A rusted, uneasy
> oblivion. I didn't hide, as I said I would. Some hand of god or primal
> instinct made me leave the roof, ask for help. It was beautiful
> up there. On the very south-west corner, the wind was amazing, and
> that late afternoon sunlight. Perfect.

> Wed Jun 17 23:35:01

It feels heavy
All those blue killjoys
in my stomach

I suppose it's alright
I have plenty of memories

6.41 a.m.

She awakens slowly. She's in a
giant metal tube. It's some kind
of scanning machine. She drifts
back into an uneasy sleep.

8.18 a.m.

A face focuses close to hers. A voice. 'What did you take?'
    Silence.
    'What did you take?' he repeats.
    Her voice comes then, outside herself, a hoarse whisper.
'Sleeping pills.'
    'What kind were they?'
    'I don't know.'
    'How many did you take?'
    'Thirty-two.'
    'Why did you take them?'
    'So I'd sleep thirty-two nights.'
    This time, he is silent.
    'Who are you?' she asks.
    'We're here to help you.'

1

She is becoming aware of her body. 'I need to go to the bathroom.'

'No, you don't. You have a catheter. It's pressing on your bladder. That's what you feel.'

'No, I really do.'

The man sighs and unstraps her hands and feet from the bed. She hadn't realized she was tied to the bed until now. She stands unsteadily and looks down at herself. She's wearing a white hospital gown with little blue flowers. No shoes. He hands her the catheter bag and escorts her to the bathroom and waits outside.

Inside, she tries to pee but can't. So she stands and looks at herself in the faux mirror. Her left eye is black, unswollen, as if face paint has been smeared around her eye. Her lips are also black and her hair wild. She doesn't recognize herself. The uneven stain on her lips disturbs her and she looks closer. When the reflection leans in, she jumps back in alarm before she remembers she's in front of a mirror. A nurse enters.

'My lips are black,' she says.

The nurse answers, 'It's the charcoal they made you eat so you'd throw up.'

I am afraid of spaces.
I hold my breath crossing
bridges, close my eyes looking
out of windows, wait don't wait
for wind on ledges.
I make lists.
Short lists.
Long lists. Sure lists.
Unsure lists. I make them
every failing second.

I don't know why
I'm sad. I know
what good I have.
I know the strength
of me. But sadness
steals my breath.
It was bad years ago.
I thought it had gone
away. I used to kill it
with poems. Then music.
Now the real vices
of oblivion. I've lost control.

I'm sorry, God, magic, love,
whoever it is I'm writing.
I don't know how to stop
my whims. They are driving me
fucking crazy.

Green White Green

The limits of my body
Become the limits of my world.

—*Kaiser Haq*

eventide, 77°F
unu nwere kom-kom
kom-kom
unu nwere kom-kom
kom-kom
– the cry of the tin can hawkers

Drums

School starts tomorrow. Real school. Not the nursery school just behind our house. I'm four years old, and at the University of Nigeria Nsukka Primary School, I'll have my own satchel and wear a uniform and carry a water bottle. Amma made my kindergarten uniform on her sewing machine. It's a dress with blue and white checkers and pointed collars. My water bottle has a long red rubber cord and ridges across its blue-moon body. It's hanging in the kitchen on a nail.

Today we made necklaces out of frangipani flowers. We have the only peach frangipani tree in town. Everyone else has white or yellow. The flowers come off the branches easily, but first we have to use the ones that have fallen on the ground. My necklace had ten flowers on lavender thread. My little sister, Simi, used yellow thread but she's only three so Amma had to help her with the needle. When I put the necklace on, the fragrance was so strong, it made me dizzy.

It's dark now and the crickets are calling. Amma has finished reading to us and she's tucking Simi in. Our twin beds are next

7

to each other and there's a wooden nightstand in between. The nightstand used to hold the Grundig tape player, the one that played classical music on big round reels while we slept, the tape flying wild at the end of the collection. Now, the Grundig is in the living room, next to the radio that plays the BBC and Voice of America in the mornings.

'Ghumai jao,' Amma whispers in Bangla, as she switches off the light and closes the door. 'Go to sleep.'

Her shadow darkens the space in the doorway and then goes away. My body is flat between the cool sheet and the springy mattress, safe and snug. But I won't sleep yet. I'm waiting for the drums. I know they're coming. They always do. The drums are for the dancers, at night, fire in the centre, in the villages that seem so far away in the day, but move closer at night.

Sometimes, the drums come into town, carried in by the juju men, the witch people. They go from compound to compound and they sing and they dance, wearing huge painted masks. I don't know if they have real faces underneath. We give them money because if we don't, it's bad luck.

The drums are so faint at first I don't even hear them. And then, just before I fall asleep, from somewhere inside the jungle, they come.

harmattan, 78°F

Pi, Pi, Pi, Pi,
Pitakwa na a kpo gi
Elu uwa si gi bia
Selense si na bugibu
Lagos emeri go Ibadan
One senseya emeri go Ibaadan
Two senseya emeri go Ibadan …
– Igbo clapping game

Red and Orange

Nsukka is a small town in a valley in southeastern Nigeria. The mornings and evenings are cool enough to wear blazers, but the afternoons are roasting. During the rainy season, there is a thunderstorm every afternoon. The sky turns black and roars. Then the rain comes.

We're in the dry season now. It's called harmattan, after the desert winds that travel thousands of miles from northern Africa all the way to the West African coast. It's not going to rain for months. The ground thins, losing its red skin to the incessant wind. Dust blows everywhere. We have to sweep twice a day or our feet leave footprints on the floor. Our lips crack and our limbs turn grey in the dry heat.

Every Sunday, my mother sits Simi and me down to write letters. We have our own little table, tucked into a corner with two chairs, one for Simi and one for me. We keep our notebooks and pencils there. Our reading books are on the other side of the room, in a bookcase as tall as me, with three shelves. It's full of Ladybird books, small and hard and easy to stack. My favourite book though isn't a Ladybird book. It's bigger, and has folktales from different countries. I like the Russian story best, about a little girl called Vasilissa and her magic doll and the witch, Baba Yaga.

Once a week, we write to our grandparents in Bangladesh on lined paper, every other line.

Dear Nana and Nanu, how are you? I am fine.
Dear Dada and Dadi, how are you? I am fine.

We draw large careful letters that hover between the lines. The letters to Nana and Nanu go to the capital city of Dhaka, to a bungalow with an overgrown garden buzzing with crows and a pond so big you can hardly see the other side. The letters to my paternal grandparents go further, to a village called Barahipur in southeastern Bangladesh.

Nanu came to visit us once. She brought bangles and toys from Bangladesh. They smelled like her, like fennel and ironed cotton. In the evenings, Simi and I played oga and other clapping games as she walked with Amma in the garden, between the allamanda bushes and the cactus plants with their thorny sprawling leaves. I could hear her saying how peaceful it was, how quiet.

It's always quiet in Nsukka. Even when the president changes and no one likes it. After two military coups, the last leader, General Obasanjo, has handed over power to a civilian. The new president's name, Shehu Shagari, sounds funny because he's from the north. All smooth rolling sounds, not the staccato rhythms of Igbo. But in our university town, nothing seems different. Only the war, the one the Igbos fought and lost, before

I was born, before my parents arrived in Nigeria, hangs like a backdrop behind everything. I don't know what it means, but it's there, the word, Biafra, as familiar as my own name.

This harmattan, Jamie Mama, my mother's younger brother, has come to visit from Ankara, Turkey where he is studying architecture. He presents Simi and me with red and orange cotton dresses, and there's a tiny button-up shirt for my brand new baby brother, Maher. Simi and I interrupt our hopscotch game straight away and run into our parents' bedroom to try on the dresses.

'Brush your hair,' my mother tells me, as she does every few hours. My hair is curly and refuses to sit neatly if it isn't tied back. I ignore her as I preen in her mirror, holding my hopscotch stone in my hand. The stone is flat on one side, so it doesn't roll around too much after it lands. The hem of my new dress barely settles around my knees before I run back outside.

After Jamie Mama leaves, Simi and I have a fight about which dress is hers and which mine. We are only a year-and-half apart, so the dress sizes are the same.

'The orange dress is mine!' I shout. 'I remember wearing it when we got them!'

Simi's face is streaked with tears. 'No, the red one is yours! The orange one is mine!'

'You're wrong! You don't remember anything. I was wearing the orange one! It is *mine.*'

We go on like this until I bully Simi into agreeing with me. This is nothing new. As the oldest, I have been getting my way for seven years now. My 'evil eye' is legendary in my family. But this time I'm right. I can see my reflection in the mirror wearing the orange dress.

Months later, while leafing through our photo albums, I

come across a polaroid photograph of our family from when Jamie Mama came to visit. We're in our front compound in front of my mother's white rose bushes. In the picture, my uncle is holding my naked baby brother high in the air and I know with hindsight that Maher is about to pee on him. My mother is sitting on the veranda steps, laughing. She has curly hair like mine, only longer, and pulled tightly into a ponytail. Her face though is like Simi's, round and open and fair.

My father is wearing that faint air of amusement he wears only in photographs. He stands head and shoulders above us all. At six feet, he is tall for a Bangladeshi; Amma almost a foot shorter than him. My uncle is only a little taller than my mother.

The ground beneath us is red and dusty, and I'm looking sullen because I hate taking pictures. My sister is standing to Jamie Mama's left, smiling her brilliant smile. She's wearing the orange dress.

In that moment, I realize memory is a treacherous thing. And I'm extra nice to Simi for a while.

first gust, 80°F
in the land of Mars
where the ladies smoke cigars
each puff they take
is enough to kill a snake
when the snake is dead
they put flowers on its head
when the flowers die
they put diamonds in its eyes
when the diamonds break, it is 1988.
– author unknown

Black Keys

Tanu is a skinny Indian girl who lives two streets away from us. She's in grade three, one above me, and her words are as sharp as her chin. I like going to her house because she has comic books about gods and goddesses and other religious stories. The comic I read and reread is about a prince called Siddhartha who gives away everything he owns, even the clothes on his back. He tears out all his hair in four handfuls, and he leaves his palace, his family, everything he knows.

Everywhere he goes, he is met with disdain or anger. People yell at him, throw things at him, drive him away from their homes. In each frame, his nakedness is obscured by something – a tree, a house, a weapon raised in rage. Still, he keeps searching, and it is long years later that he finds what he's looking for, while sitting serene under a tree, and a light spreads out like a fan all around him.

Sometimes Tanu and I watch TV with her mother. Her mother loves watching Hindi films. The films have a lot of singing and dancing so you don't have to understand Hindi. Today the film we're watching stops halfway through. I look at Tanu's mother, but she's already on her way to the kitchen.

'Intermission!' she calls over her shoulder, as the word appears on the TV screen.

I'm sorry because Tanu wants to leave and I think I was even starting to understand the plot. Maybe it was the obvious gestures and expressions of the actors, or knowing Bangla helped me more than I realized. I suppose it doesn't matter how I understand, only if I do. There's no in-between to understanding.

The only time I see Tanu is when we play in the evenings, because there isn't any inter-grade interaction at our school. Her father, like mine, is a professor at the University of Nigeria, Nsukka. Practically everyone in my school has a parent who teaches at the university or practices medicine at the university hospital. I have many classmates, Nigerian and foreign both, who holiday abroad, whose parents I address as Dr so-and-so, who's hoping to go to England or America for university.

'I know a good song,' Tanu tells me one day when we are playing Monopoly at my house.

'What is it called?' I ask, moving my metal iron token down the board. I love the iron. I always make sure I choose it. Simi prefers the shoe. Tanu has the horse. I don't know why she chose it, because it's too tall and falls over easily.

'I don't know.'

'Who sings it?'

'I don't know,' she says again, impatiently. 'Do you want to learn it or not?'

'Yes. Of course.'

My mother enters the room. 'Girls, clean up the living room. Your fathers are coming to play bridge soon.'

'Amma! We're in the middle of a game,' I protest.

'I didn't say you had to stop playing. You can take the board to your room,' she says mildly.

'Let's stop,' Tanu says. 'I can teach you the song. And it's not because I'm losing because I'm not. I have Park Lane *and* Mayfair.'

She's lying but I want to learn the song, so I start stacking up the Chance and Community Chest cards. The last song we were obsessed with was a nonsense rhyme with a hypnotic rhythm about a land called Mars. Tanu's song sounds similar, but it has no words. You're supposed to play it on a harmonium or piano, but we don't have either. She says it's a snake charmer's song. Whatever it is, we both love the sound of it. The melody is constantly in our heads, on the tips of our tongues. Even Simi knows it, though she doesn't often play with us.

Some evenings, Tanu and I play tennis at the courts past the stadium. We have wooden rackets, which we have to keep screwed onto racks when we're not using them or they'll warp from the weather. One day, walking up Ako Okweli Street with our rackets, we hear the clinking sounds of a piano. It's an unusual sound in our quiet little town. There's only the roar of the occasional car and the birds and crickets and children. Once, the wails of mourners at a funeral. Always the wind.

'Where is it coming from?' I ask Tanu.

'I don't know. Let's find out.'

She scrambles over a dried-up ditch not waiting for me to follow. The winds converge as we scale a miniature hill, the weeds waving, higher than our heads. At the top of the hill, a hedge foils us, until I spy a space in it, low to the ground, between two thin trunks, with just enough room to crawl through.

We emerge behind a row of one-storey buildings. It's the music department. Someone is playing a piano inside. Tanu and I look at each other with the same thought, but conflicting reactions.

'They may have an empty practice room,' she says.

'What if we get caught?' I ask.

She ignores me and walks on. Heart racing, I follow. One of the buildings consists of two long rows of practice rooms with a corridor down the centre. Some of the rooms are occupied with people playing piano, but either their doors are closed or they are too busy to notice us. We sneak into one of the practice rooms undetected.

We spend the next few weeks banging out the tune to the snake charmer's song. It's clear from the beginning that almost none of the white keys sounds right. In fact, it only sounds good when we use mostly black keys.

When Tanu is bored with our sessions, I return to the practice rooms alone, to try and play parts of other songs. There aren't any local radio stations in Nsukka, only the BBC and the Voice of America, and we don't have a TV. So my musical knowledge is limited to what I've heard on those two stations and my mother's tapes.

I pound out parts of 'Cecilia' by Simon and Garfunkel, 'Thriller' by Michael Jackson, and 'In the Ghetto' by Elvis Presley. There's another song I heard on the radio called 'The Maneater' by Hall and Oates, but it's too fast for me to play. I know the Elvis songs by heart because my mother plays them when she comes back from teaching Economics at the girls' secondary school. The Grundig spirals out his voice as we pace up and down the cool concrete veranda in front of our house. The veranda has three open sides covered with netting and it's painted a blood-red colour that I love.

'I first dreamt about you when I was in Libya,' my mother tells me, ruffling my hair. 'I flew there from Bangladesh to join your father after we got married. But it wasn't even Bangladesh then. It was still East Pakistan and I was in West Pakistan, in university at Lahore, when your Nanu wrote to tell me to come home.'

'Why did she want you to come home?' I ask.

'She said she had found a husband for me, that he was tall and good-looking and educated, that he lived abroad. But to me, it mattered only that she approved of him. So I left Lahore and went back to Dhaka to get married.'

I try to think of my father as a young man looking for a wife. The only context I have for this is in the Nigerian folk tales I've read, like the brave young farmer who has to be clever and kind in order to win the hand of his beloved and defeat the trickster gods. But to me, Abbu is ever the professor, with accented authority in his voice and stature. He is a scientist and a devout Muslim. He is my strict and articulate father.

My mother is still telling her story. 'After the wedding in Bangladesh, I went to Tripoli. Such a beautiful city by the sea.'

'Were you afraid?' Simi asks. 'Of the sea, I mean?' I know she's asking this because she's afraid of waves.

'No, but I do remember something scary. It was my first night in Tripoli and it was very late and we were already in bed. Suddenly, there was a loud crashing sound, like bombs bursting, and it woke us up. Your Abbu said it was nothing, that Libyans liked to set off firecrackers for weddings and other celebrations.

So we went back to sleep, but in the morning, when we switched on the radio, the announcer said there had been a coup in Libya and General Gaddafi had taken over power!'

Elvis is singing, 'And look the other way? Well, the world turns ...'

'You got the Elvis music in Tripoli, right?' Simi adds.

'Yes, I did. You remember! I got bored sitting at home all day while your Abbu was teaching at the university, so I got a job at the local radio station. It was just a few hours a day, but it was a lot of fun, playing whatever music was popular. I taped some of it before I left, like the Elvis songs.'

'And then you came to Nigeria and had me,' I say.

'Well, first we went to Bangladesh, and it was finally Bangladesh then. It was the summer of 1972, just after the war. We were there for a few months, and then we came to Nigeria. By then, you were in my tummy,' she gestures towards me. Her sari is a billowing brown-and-green Georgette fabric. 'I carried you here. So you're our Nigerian baby, because you were born in Nigeria.'

'And I'm the Bangladeshi baby,' Simi says. 'Because you went back to Bangladesh to have me.'

This part is a familiar story. We've been telling it for as long as I can remember.

'Yes. And this one is the American baby,' Amma says, chucking Maher under the chin.

He laughs and swats the portent air with his chubby arms. Outside the veranda, the trade winds are hazing the heavy air with dust. Inside, the Elvis tape is done, the reel spinning in silence.

Amma says she went to America to have Maher because the hospitals in America are better than in Nigeria or Bangladesh.

But I think it's because she wanted us to have three different homes. Then we wouldn't fight about where we were from. We could each have a place to call our own, or all three if we shared.

'Sing, Amma!' Simi says.

Amma knows many Bangla songs from growing up in Dhaka. Nursery rhymes and childhood verses, songs by Rabindranath Tagore and Nazrul, folk songs.

She sings, 'Mono mor meghero shongi, ure choley digdigontero pane, nihshshimo shunney, srabono borshono songeete, rimijhim rimijhim rimijhim …'

It's one of my favourites, a rising melody about the rain by Tagore.

'Now you dance,' she says, 'to "*Babu salam bare*".'

'*Babu Salam*' is a dancing song and Amma has taught us the dance steps for it.

'Go on,' she says, taking Maher from my arms, and suddenly my arms feel light.

I look at Simi and we nod in unison, raising our right arms above us in the falling dark.

Amma starts singing, 'Babu salam bare, ah, ah, ah …'

We dance forward, bowing as we go.

shade cool, 81°F
Nile, Niger, Senegal, Congo,
Orange, Limpopo, Zambezi
Azikiwe, Awolowo, Tafawa Balewa
Onyocha wepu aka Nigeria
– Nigerian children's song

Standing in the Sun

Obiageli is taunting me again. I don't know why she dislikes me. Maybe she's jealous of my first rank in grade four. Or that I get to hold my best friend Nneka's hand as we wander through the primary school compound during break. Or it's because I'm an onyocha, a foreigner, in Nigeria.

One onyocha story goes: the first European visitors to Nigeria caused a stir with their closed-toed shoes. Where were their toes? No one in his or her right mind wears closed shoes in tropical Africa. Your feet would rot. But the onyochas forged on, seemingly toeless.

I stub my brown sandals into the hard red dirt and watch Obiageli. We're standing under a tree, the shade so thick it's almost dark under the leaves, despite the blazing light on the outskirts of the shade. Smaller and paler than most of my classmates, I am even more diminished beside Obiageli. She also has a reputation for being a little unstable, a little wild.

Her teeth flash. 'Tufiakwa!' she says, running her fingers underneath her armpits and then snapping them in my face.

This means shame on you, shame on your family. Family

20

insults are the height of mockery and everyone uses them, if sparingly. But Obiageli never seems to ration her supply.

'Waka, onyocha!' She raises her palm at me, fingers spread, her palm pink against her skin.

I don't quite know what this insult means except that it's less severe than the last. Three horizontal raised ridges highlight each of her cheekbones and smaller vertical ones divide her forehead down the middle. This is not the first time I've noticed Obiageli's scars. There aren't many local children in our school. The large majority has middle to upper-class Nigerians parents who were educated abroad. There is a smattering of foreign families from South Asia and Europe. The university is one of the best in the country and the town is enclosed by a wall with armed guards at the gates.

Twenty years after Nigeria's independence from Great Britain, our little English-medium school is rooted in Anglocentrism. Our open-toed sandals may be one concession to the daily blazing heat, but we are required to don pristinely white socks under them. Within a few months, these socks will be indelibly stained with the red dust that covers everything. The blue and white chequered shirt that all the schoolgirls wear is overlaid with a thick navy pinafore, styled with pleats. The boys also wear chequered shirts and formal shorts in the same thick fabric as our pinafores. This is the latest in English fashion, from decades ago, and unsuited to either of our two seasons: dry heat and wet heat.

Obiageli's pinafore is wrinkled and a darker shade of blue than the prescribed navy, both indicators of lower economic status. Not having the right sized chequers on your shirt, wearing a lighter or darker shade of blue, wrinkled uniforms, worn sandals, no water bottle, these are all signs. But how much money your family has is not a high rung in the ladder of popularity and success. There are other, more pressing, differences to think about, like the colour of my skin.

I spend a lot of time outside. I figure that the longer I'm in the sun, the darker and thus less different my skin will be from that of my black friends. No matter that they are darker than dark, that their skin shines so that I can almost see my own reflection on their bodies.

'Gorilla woman!' Obiageli has turned to English barbs. She's referring to my arms and legs, which are covered with more hair than any Nigerian child's. The English words, while familiar, are also more irritating.

'Koottar bachcha!' I spit out the first Bangla insult that comes into my head. It's one my mother has used on us, but I don't think about what it means until the words leave my mouth.

Dog's child …

She leans into me threateningly. 'Wot doz dat mean?'

I think about it. Have I insulted Obiageli's mother or father? But wouldn't that mean my mother was insulting herself when she said it? Somehow, this Bangla profanity seems worse than yelling 'Tufiakwa' and snapping one's fingers in another's face.

'Notting,' I say.

I see Nneka walking towards us and relax. Obiageli sees my visible relief and turns around. Nneka is even taller than Obiageli. She is also good in school, a much more important rung on that ladder of prestige. But the fact that she's brave is the only thing I care about right now.

'Wot iz eet?' Nneka asks Obiageli. 'Wot do you want wit ha?'

It's Obiageli's turn to say nothing. Nneka takes my hand and we leave the cool of the shade and walk away.

The half-castes are the only ones who have it worse than

the foreigners. The foreigners can't help being foreigners, but being half-Nigerian is like being a traitor, betraying the black race. I tell myself that as much as I want my skin to be darker, I wouldn't want to have just half-Nigerian blood. I want all or nothing. It might be too hard to almost belong. Not belonging, on the other hand, is cut and dried, an easy place to find.

Aidan is a half: half-Canadian, half-Nigerian, and he has grey eyes. The first time we see him is in French class. When he walks in, he looks blind, the light trapped tragically in the ash of his eyes, rendering them weak or useless. It's not just me with this theory. At break, a curious group circles him, staring at his contracting pupils in the sunlight. We make him prove that he can see through his eyes by asking him to identify things in the landscape.

It's true though that Aidan beat all the Nigerians in a running event, even if his victory comes in long distance, not in the glory sprints. When he wins his race at our annual Sports Day event, there is no one else on the track with him. Everyone else has dropped out hundreds of metres before. When he crosses the finish line for the last time, the stadium goes wild. From then on, it seems his half-ness is tempered by that triumph. He is a runner first, a sportsman, rungs higher than skin colour on the ladder of standing.

Liam is half-Irish, half-Nigerian. His skin is the colour of milky tea and his hair is a tangle of loose curls. Everyone hates him, Nigerians and foreigners alike, because he's beautiful, charming, and can speak the local tribal language, Igbo, without a trace of an accent. Even I hate him, and as a foreigner, I have many reasons to understand.

It's not fair to say hate. Jealousy is closer to the truth. After all, if we hated Liam, would the boys ask him to play soccer on the scrabby fields? Or watch him secretly, as the girls do, when he tells rough-and-tumble stories to his friends? Still, Liam faces derision at every wrong move, which I think is worse than being mostly ignored like I am.

'Look at Liam's new shoes. I am going to make wata' on dem.'

'Mba, don't make him cry. Besides, he will jost get his vice chancella' fatha' to buy him anotha peh.'

It won't matter if Liam tells them his father was never vice chancellor. The taunts will continue, and I will keep standing in the sun.

bow echo, 73°F

> Me knows the trick I'm trying to play
> That time trick where everything heals
>
> But me is just lying in wait so I forget
> And me will rise again out of shadow and rage
>
> I am so afraid of dying. Me cannot wait for it.

9.56 a.m.

She still doesn't know where she is. Only that there are mad people all around. She can't have anything made of glass or with strings. Fifteen minutes on the pay phone. No visitors in her room.

Psychiatric Medical Care Unit Patient Behavior Guidelines
*You will receive one contact person per shift and you will deal primarily with that one contact person for that entire shift. This contact person will act as the official liaison between you and the rest of the staff.

She asks Wendy, the nurse assigned to her, for paper and a pen and gets old printer paper with rows of holes down either side and a blunt pencil. Patients don't get pens. She hates writing with pencil. It never looks precise, and it doesn't slice into the paper like pen and ink. Perched on her lumpy twin bed, she writes.

If you weren't crazy before you entered this place, then you'd be crazy after, ill anyway, surrounded by this madness, sometimes manic, sometimes lethargic, always disturbing.

She stops and looks at the smudgy marks. She should work on her penmanship. Wendy looks in. She likes her. She seems sturdy, understanding.

'How are you feeling?'

She doesn't look up. 'I'm fine.'

She's hoping they find a chemical imbalance in her head that can be fixed with medicine, because otherwise she cannot reconcile why she would want to take this lovely body and silver mind to hell. Is she spoilt? Is she weak? Is she stupid? Is she a hypocrite? Is she afraid? Is she doing this to be cool? To be troubled? To have a cause?

```
              I said once to God, don't help me
                      or at least do the opposite
                       of what you're doing now
              because whatever you were doing before
                                    didn't help

                             I said once to God,
                     some bright September afternoon
              and it's some bright September afternoon
              now, and I'm trapped inside a promise
```

blizzard, 9°F
it's dark and warm inside the room
it's almost safe, it's always doomed
look just once behind your heart
all the pieces come apart

Judo Lessons

I'm standing, precarious, on the table in the dining room, reaching high above my head towards my father's books. I've already read one or two mystery novels. This time, the book I pull out says *Erotica* on the cover. I jump down and run to my room. I have always loved reading, but my collection of British Enid Blyton books and American Nancy Drew stories aren't enough to satisfy my appetite. So I've turned to my father's collection.

My family has come to America for one year. Abbu is on sabbatical, a word I find romantic and exciting, and it has brought us here, to a tiny warm apartment in Pittsburgh, going to primary school with pink and white American children. After the school year is over, we will return to Nigeria.

Erotica turns out to be a collection of short stories. I don't understand much of it, but I keep reading. There are stories about men and women, men and men, women and women, women and boys, men and girls, people and animals, and more. I have no basis for judging which stories are wrong and which aren't. The story of the sleepy socialite who gets licked to orgasm by a dog and the old woman who has sex with the teenage boy by the abandoned train station and the husband who tenderly shaves his wife – all embed in my mind with the same authority. Anyway, it's my father's book, and that lends it immediate credence. He has such moral and adult superiority that I have never been able to fault him in the slightest. The only other thing I can think of is it was a gift, but then wouldn't he have given it away if he didn't want it?

Whenever I hear someone coming near my room, I shove the book under my mattress. In between school and play and sleep, I read. Sometimes, I forgo sleep to read under my blanket with a torchlight. It takes me a month to read most of the stories. Then, one afternoon, I run into my room and slide my hand under the mattress, and there's nothing. The book is gone.

I don't think of the erotica book when I meet Elly, even though she is my first sexual encounter. There weren't any stories about little girls touching so I didn't connect erotica to myself. Elly has coarse pubic hair. I don't know whether it's supposed to be like that because I haven't grown any yet, but it seems strange, and so I keep my fumblings to her butt, which is so smooth and round. We don't touch each other's breasts at all, because they're flat and don't feel like much.

Every afternoon after school, Elly and I tumble around in an empty unlocked apartment we found in our building, and we play house. It's too cold to play outside, a snowstorm having come in a rush one night and garlanded everything. The tops of the snow banks have delicate ice veneers that crackle and crumble with a touch of my gloved hand.

Elly's younger brother and Simi play our children, but we get tired of parenting and lock ourselves in the bedroom that has a bed and a dresser, and we jump on the bed until we're tired, and flop down and feel each other up, giggling when our kids get bored and bang on the door, asking us if they can come in.

But it's our landlord, Pep, who holds even more sway. Pep gives judo lessons to all the kids in the complex. There's a big padded room beside his basement apartment where we practice every week. Afterwards, we flood his apartment to drink Coke and feed his fish. The fish in his aquarium are brighter than flowers. Since my family has never had pets, it's the first time I get to feed a creature other than my little brother. I always sprinkle in extra fish food when Pep isn't looking. And since I'm not allowed soda pop at home, the Cokes are a treat.

We sit in Pep's living room, on the shag-covered couch, sipping Coke, chatting as if we're grown-ups at a party, not fifth graders in corduroys and T-shirts. Elly is the one who gets up and goes into Pep's bedroom. When she pushes open the bedroom door, only I'm brave enough to follow. And when I see the waterbed, I'm glad I came with her. I've never seen a waterbed before.

Elly clambers onto it with easy familiarity. She lurches and falls, laughing. I can't resist. I join her. There is something about the uneven motion that makes the place not like a bedroom at all, more like an amusement park, or a science museum. We bounce and roll and dive, and I don't know how long Pep has been standing in the doorway before he speaks. I jump off at his admonition, but Elly remains unrepentantly prostrate on the crumpled sheets. He shakes his head and goes back to the living room.

But Elly isn't the one who finds Pep's closet. I am. The closet I can't stay away from. The one I go to even on days we don't have judo. It's a tiny room, with a single naked light bulb swinging from the ceiling, and instead of clothes, the shelves are lined with sex magazines.

I know it's wrong to be there, standing under the wavering shadows, but I can't help myself. It's not even that I like the pictures so much, but I want to know what's inside each magazine. The redhead with such large breasts that her willing tongue can reach them, the laughing black woman with the afro tied to a clothesline, and other women with their legs so wide you can see straight into that deep wet pinkness. It's a complete mystery each time, every page turn a guilty revelation.

It's why I don't blame Pep when he comes into the closet. I have come on my own after all, to satisfy this relentless thing acting through my body. In the beginning, he doesn't do much at all. Rubbing and squeezing my nipples through my clothes while I flip through the magazines. It doesn't hurt and I can even ignore it, take it as payment for my curiosity.

It's only later that he tries more, unzipping my jeans, unbuttoning my shirt. I push his hands away each time, and they move back up, easily spanning my chest. He doesn't ever say anything, or go further than I let him. He knows I might not come back otherwise.

It's almost the end of Abbu's sabbatical when we hear the whispers about Elly. They say she is a bad girl and we shouldn't play with her. We find out that she's accused Pep of rape. Some parents say she said this because she's black, which doesn't make sense because Pep is black too. No one thinks he might have something to do with it. Not our gregarious beloved landlord who gives judo lessons and soda pop to all the kids in the complex. It must be Elly crying wolf, Elly with her ready mouth and taunting words and unapologetic ardour. And so she becomes a stranger in my eyes, despite all our afternoons in frozen sunlight in the empty apartment, touching each other in breathless silence.

The last time I see Elly, my family is climbing the stairs to our third floor apartment. It's late spring, but I haven't gotten used to the changeling weather, so I'm still wearing my puffy winter jacket with a hood framing my face. My shoulders are wet with rain. Elly is wearing a T-shirt and jeans, standing on the second floor landing, her hands on her hips. My parents give no sign of recognizing her, but I am acutely aware of her presence. I haven't seen her in weeks because our judo lessons are over, and anyway, she's been scarce because of the scandal.

'Hey,' she says, when I get close.

I don't think I glance up high enough to see her face. I know I say nothing back. I walk past her, and on into the rest of my life.

I pledge to Nigeria, my caw-awn-tree
to be faitful, loyal, and aw-aw-nest
to sahv Nigeria wit all my strent
to defend ha unity
and uphold ha ona and glo-oh-ry
so help me, God.
– the Nigerian Pledge of Allegiance

Tyger Tyger

We have started to learn William Blake's old ode to the tiger. We chant with enthusiasm, if not nuance. The heavy rhyme and meter drown any sense that might have accompanied the unfamiliar words. We are too concerned with getting the sounds in the right order to think about what the poem means.

The University of Nigeria Primary School operates under an almost militaristic regime in its ample tree-demarcated square in the middle of town. Even the classrooms, simple one-floor structures arranged in sets of three, resemble barracks. Mr Eze runs grade 6B with an iron fist and a cane made of the stiffest branch our class monitor, Nnamdi, can find in the brambles outside. No questions are allowed in class: only answers or silence.

We have three weeks to learn this poem: ten minutes at the end of each school day. Every few days, Mr Eze will add a new verse to the right side of the blackboard in his perfect and precise penmanship. At the end of the three weeks, he will erase the poem from the board and we will recite it by heart in front of the entire primary school at Assembly.

On the first day, we wait silently inside the classroom, while Mr Eze fumes over his last cane, broken and useless at his feet. Outside, Nnamdi is smoothing the branch he has broken off a tree and is walking reluctantly back to the classroom. When he enters, Mr Eze walks swiftly and heavily over to the door and takes the cane from his hand. Our monitor is good-looking, tall for his age, taller than even most of the secondary school boys. This allows him a natural authority and that, coupled with respectable school marks, makes him an obvious choice for the coveted position of class monitor. He slips into his chair with an easy grace, unusual for his size and age, and hunches over his worn wooden desk at the front of the row nearest the door. I watch him from the back of the classroom as Mr Eze waves his new cane at us to begin.

and wot sholda and wot aht
cood twist de sinews of dy haht

As half the class stumbles over the word 'sinews,' Mr Eze raises his cane and snaps it down on Nnamdi's desk. His bald head is shiny with sweat and droplets are forming above his forehead.

'Silence!' he roars. 'See-news, not sigh-news. How many times will we haf to do dis?'

He starts down the aisle and asks each person in succession to pronounce the word. A slight deviation results in a sharp and painful rap on the back of a hand or an arm or back. Mr Eze seems to be in a generous mood this time. We spent most of the last poem on our knees on the rough cement floor with rising welts on our backs, legs, and butts. Still, I pray for the break bell before he gets to the third row, and me, and within moments, I hear a deliberate clang.

We pour out of the classroom into the light and space of the sprawling schoolyard. The back fields are filling with boys setting up soccer matches. I head over to the trees by the empty basketball courts to do what all the girls do, which is play clapping games. There are many clapping games, but the one we never fail to play at least once a day, rain or shine, is oga. Oga is a complicated dancing and clapping game that involves trying to match balletic foot positions with whoever is leading the game. Match one of six possible foot placements with the leader as she faces off with each girl in the semi-circle and you become the leader. Everyone has a different dance and clap style for oga. Mine is low-key and short, nothing fancy. But I am as addicted to this game as anyone else. We would play for hours if we could, our hands clapping a ceaseless rhythm under the ironed blue sky.

In the second week of our practice, the headmistress pays grade 6B a visit. Our stout teacher waves us into immediate silence as he stands in the doorway and speaks in low deferential tones to her. Although they are the same height, her crisp and colourful head-dress makes her seem much taller than him. Mr Eze returns from his conference with a renewed fervour. Our last poem, 'Journey of the Magi,' set a standard with its complicated referential lines, and the headmistress is expecting nothing less from our next recital. We start chanting again.

> *wot de hamma, wot de chain*
> *in wot fonace was dye brain*

wot de anveel, wot dread grasp
dae its deadly terros clasp

We all wonder what a 'de-anveel' is. Even if we did know, it wouldn't help. The rest of the poem is a mystery. Was the tiger alight? Was it in hell? But at least it's more exciting than our last poem. That one was boring on top of being incomprehensible. We never figured out what a Magi was and that was just the title. 'The Tyger' at least sounds dangerous, full of motion and dark light.

when de stas true down dae speeyas
and watad hevun wit dae teeyas

In the third week, we are almost enjoying ourselves. We sway with the rigid and swinging meter of each verse, the sounds stabbing out of our mouths with force and a measure of confidence. Even Mr Eze seems pleased with our progress. The canings have been infrequent and our regular subject material has been meted with a lighter touch.

Luckily, we are all used to memorizing. It's the way we learn everything, from mathematics to English to science to history. And at home, every weekend, my mother teaches us surahs from the Quran as part of our Islamic education. Simi and I each have surah notebooks, with a dozen or so prayers copied down carefully in both Arabic and English. Some are four or five lines and others are almost a page long, and we've memorized them, one by one.

When the three weeks are up, our class lines up in the Assembly grounds in front of the headmistress's office. Assembly starts off each school day. Grades four through six are arrayed in a square horseshoe and the headmistress stands in the opening facing us.

The sun is beating down, but we don't notice. The morning classes, kindergarten and grades one through three, have just been let out and they are streaming out of class, some through the tall hedges and down the road, others into the red dirt parking lot to meet their waiting parents.

We stand quietly until the headmistress appears. My pinafore is ironed, pleats perfect. I want to tug at my shirt collar but it's almost time, so I don't move. She waves her arm at us, and in unison, we launch into the Pledge of Allegiance.

The sun glares on. I don't have to touch the top of my head to know my scalp is radiating heat or that Nnamdi's won't be, his tight black curls unperturbed.

Mr Eze leads his class to the front of the Assembly where the fifty-two of us stand in five neat rows beside the headmistress. I stand in the front row, as per height. Our teacher smiles at us, and for a moment I am so stunned at this rare display of warmth that I almost forget the first word, '*Ty-ga* …'

It is a good starting line, better than, '*A cold coming we had of it* …' from the Magi poem, which seems weak and anticlimactic. And I don't think any of us really understands the cold. Cold is only in the British books we read, with pictures of snow-covered two-storey houses with children wearing so many clothes that we feel choked just looking at them. The tiger, though, is a creature of the tropics, lauded in folk tales, pictured in textbooks, its cousins trapped and wilting in our little town zoo. The tiger, we understand.

opacity, 83°F
the heat makes its mark
we whisper, we swear
we lift our shiny faces
to the trembling air

Hieroglyphics

Mrs Okonkwor hasn't finished her lesson on the human skeleton. She's chalking names of various bones on the board. But it's almost 4.30 p.m., and we have started putting away our science books, and placing our French books on top of our worn wooden desks. She doesn't notice until Onyeabo lets the lid of his desk slip and slam shut.

'Wot ah you doing? Onyeabo, weh eez yoh science book?' Mrs Okonkwor asks, finally noticing the furtive classroom activity.

Onyeabo smiles nervously as he places his French notebook with great care on his desk. 'Mista Chukwuma's class eez next, Madahm.'

She sighs, 'Oh, I ondastand. French class.'

She puts down the chalk, claps the white dust off her hands, and ends her lesson. After she walks out, a silence settles over us. The glass window panes are missing, but the air seems reluctant to enter. I hastily leaf through my French notes, some of it borrowed as I missed class yesterday because of a cold.

Learning French in Nigeria is like learning hieroglyphics. We are memorizing sound and letter combinations, but I can't

37

understand what I'm saying, let alone decipher the phrases
Mr Chukwuma barks at us every class. The language has been
part of my curriculum for the last three years, starting in grade
four into secondary school. But the words we painstakingly
pronounced back then are as mysterious now.

JO-ma-pell Ngozi. CO-mon-TALLay-VOO.

This is my first year in secondary school after finishing
grade six at the primary school next door. We have switched
from using grades to forms, so I'm in form 1D. The bell ringer
is in form three, two years above me. At 4.30 p.m., I see him
emerge from the opposite side of the school courtyard. He starts
ringing the bell with a steady rhythm, signalling the beginning
of the next class.

The University of Nigeria Secondary School is right
beside the primary school, but the two schools have separate
classrooms, staffing, and morning assembly. Forms one through
four (grades seven to ten) are housed in a rectangle of buildings
with a tiled courtyard in the centre. Otherwise, it isn't very
different from the primary school where Simi is now in grade
five, two grades below me. There are still too many students per
class, barely enough desks and chairs, and never enough paper.

Mr Chukwuma enters our room noisily. At once, the class
monitor, Liam, raps on his desk three times.

We rise in unison and chant, 'Good aftanoon, Mista
Chukwuma!'

He laughs his booming laugh and says, 'Bonjour, mes élèves!'

He pauses to put his books down on the teacher's desk and
without further ado commands Nneka, who is sitting in the
front of the first row, 'From yestaday, what eez de French wod
fo *lazy*?'

Judging from the look on her face, Mr Chukwuma probably

forgot to teach us the French word for lazy. I send her a silent sympathetic look. Nneka and I are still fast friends. Her loyalty is single-minded, and she's the only one who regularly challenges my first rank in class.

Mr Chukwuma tells her to kneel on the floor beside her desk and moves on to the student behind her. Aidan doesn't know the word either and he kneels unbidden. I rack my brains and can't come up with the word. But there are thirty-three students before me. Someone has to know this word before he gets to me. None of us is worried about the kneeling. That's merely the scarlet letter. The real punishment comes after, when Mr Chukwuma has had a few minutes to think about what he'd like to do to us this time.

He's starting on my row, and still no one has come up with the word. More than half of Form 1D is kneeling on the concrete ground. And then, a miracle: someone says the word. *Paraso.* I write it down hurriedly in my notebook, not bothering to think about how it might be spelled. The rest of us are saved!

Mr Chukwuma turns away from us, muttering under his breath, 'Mes élèves sont paresseux.'

I know he is contemplating his punishment for the kneeling students. Hearing our class's audible murmur of relief, he wheels back toward us. This time, the silence descends as fast as the crack of his stick on Onyeabo's desk.

He shouts, 'Get out! All of you!'

We jolt and tilt the wooden desks and chairs as we struggle to get out of the room. Mr Chukwuma stands by the door and wields his thin whip without mercy. I manage to escape with a few weals on my legs. Liam is not so lucky, I notice with private satisfaction.

Outside, the light is so bright as to be opaque, fading the

landscape around us. We shift as minimally as we can, nursing welts and scratches. Mr Chukwuma stands in the doorway looking out, tapping his stick against the white cement wall.

He says authoritatively, 'Go and dig a beeg gabage ditch, six feet by six feet by six feet, in de field outside de school compound, behind de principal's office.'

Liam speaks up, 'Bot sah, we dog dat ditch last week.'

Mr Chukwuma is not pleased with his own oversight. He pauses and then says, 'You know de tall grass in de field by de capenta's shed. I want eet no mo than two inches high. And no one can go home onteel eet eez done! Now go!'

The problem is that we have no tools, no machetes, nothing. The carpenter has long locked his shed and gone home. Nneka borrows a pen knife from an older sympathetic student who walks by our sorry lot. Chuma scavenges a broken machete without a handle from somewhere in the primary school. The rest of us make do with pulling out or tearing the grass with our hands under the blazing sun. I work beside Nneka, my fingers getting dirtier and sorer by the minute. It takes us a long time.

When I get home, I'm ravenous and exhausted. Simi has been home for hours, Maher longer, as the nursery school lets out the earliest. My parents say little about my late arrival, even less about the physical punishments meted out with regularity at our school. They usually only check to see that the grades on my report card are good. It matters less how that comes about. It might be that Abbu's own British-colonized school in pre-partition rural India and Amma's education in East Pakistan's Dhaka were similar in teaching style to my university campus school in Nsukka, despite the huge gaps in geography, culture, and economics between these three places. In any case, the

uniforms are uniform. Amma told me there was a school in
Dhaka when she was growing up whose students dressed almost
identically to us, right down to the blue and white chequered
shirts, navy pinafores, and shorts.

The next time we have science class, Mrs Okonkwor
enters the room with her hair threaded. A dozen spines of
hair wound with black thread arch up towards the centre of
her scalp in a curved geometric sculpture. I love hair styles that
use thread. Straightened hair looks strange to me and braids
aren't fashionable. Using thread, on the other hand, is high
maintenance, glossy, stylish. I wish I could do it to my hair but
the thread wouldn't stay on long, and despite being curly, my
hair isn't strong or stiff enough to form the elaborate patterns.

There's also a school rule holding me back: everyone, boy
or girl, must have short hair. The foreigners, especially the
Indian Sikhs, are begrudgingly exempt from this rule about
short hair, but it wouldn't do to draw attention to an eccentric
hairstyle. There's an older Indian girl who lived at the end of
the road when we used to live on Odim Street. Vipul had a
braid that reached the back of her knees in one thick gleaming
black plait. Every evening, Simi and I would watch her walk up
and down Odim Street, her four feet of hair silking back and
forth behind her. I wonder how long her hair was when she
was in school and if she ever caught trouble for it.

'Class, I haf decided it eez time fo a test,' Mrs Okonkwor
announces.

The rest of the class groans, but I'm secretly happy because
I've already memorized the bones of the skeleton. Mrs
Okonkwor counts out forty-two sheets of paper and divides
them into stacks, placing each stack on the front desk of each
row. The papers are peeled off and passed down each row.

When I take mine, I revel for a moment in the clean white sheet. Paper is perennially in short supply, so we fill up our notebooks front to back, cover to cover. In primary school, one especially deficient year, I spent an afternoon erasing my penciled notebook from the previous grade to use for the next.

But something is wrong. The paper I've been given is completely blank. There's no drawing of the skeleton. I have a sinking feeling. Unless Mrs Okonkwor is going to test us on something other than the skeletal system, or maybe she's planning on giving us the unfathomable task of both drawing the skeleton *and* labelling each of its bones.

Sure enough, it's exactly what I fear. Our class is petrified into silence. I'm sure most of my classmates don't know the names of the bones, let alone where they are located in the body. Even with my rigorous studying, I'm only vaguely aware of the latter.

Our teacher leaves us to stew in our misery and wanders outside into the sunny courtyard. From the front of my row, Onyeabo watches her retreating form, his half-open mouth looking more helpless than usual. I look around. No one has started and the minutes are ticking. I have to do something, write something, fill up that glaring blankness. I press my sharpened pencil to the page and begin.

When the excruciating hour is over, Mrs Okonkwor asks me to collect the papers and take them to the teachers' room while she goes to her car to collect a book. It's an honour to be chosen to collect the tests, but I cannot appreciate it because I am so distraught at my performance.

The colonial school system in Nsukka is rigid and difficult, involving liberal amounts of rote memorizing and corporal punishment. In some ways, this has given us an academic advantage. I learnt geometry at age eight and my spoken and written English is pitch perfect. But ask me a logic or analytical question, and I'm lost, unable to even clarify a request because talking back is strictly forbidden.

Eight years of this and a talent for regurgitation mean I've mastered the system. I've been at the top of my class for years and, more importantly to my parents, I've achieved the highest marks possible in almost every subject. But this unexpected science test may have spoiled my perfect record. Academics is the one way I can distinguish myself, so this failure is not something I can internalize easily. The space I've carved out to stand on, my very shadow, shrinks.

Disconsolate, I collect the papers and walk down the narrow hall to the teachers' room. The teachers' room is off-limits to students and so I stand on the doorstep until one of the teachers waves me in.

'Dees ah Missus Okonkwor's paypas,' I say, handing them over to a teacher I don't recognize. She probably teaches one of the higher forms. The woman takes the exam sheets from me. As I'm walking away, she calls to me.

'Is Mrs Okonkwor still in your classroom?' she asks in Igbo.

I shake my head, about to tell her she's gone to her car, but unsure if the Igbo words are right or if I should just say it in English.

'Did you even understand what I asked?' she asks.

I stare at her wondering if I've misunderstood.

'It's a pity,' she continues in Igbo, turning to another teacher. 'They come to our country and they cannot learn our language.'

She looks at me and says, 'Is it not true?'

It's true. Our school makes no significant effort to teach Igbo as a second or even first language, and most of the foreign children don't know more than a smattering of words. I know of only one foreigner who is fluent, an Indian girl in form three, whose father teaches mathematics at the university. Matu learnt to speak Igbo from her nanny. Comfort, the nanny who took care of us when Simi and I were younger, knew English perfectly and enjoyed speaking it. Now I wish she hadn't been so fluent.

However, I understand more than just a smattering of Igbo. I know what this teacher is saying and I'm determined to prove her wrong. But I'm so nervous, even the word, *mba*, no, sticks in my throat. I end up only shaking my head once again.

The teacher laughs and shoos me out of the room into the hot still air.

coalescence, 84°F

oyo yo oyo
oyo yo oyo
augustina a muta nwa
o muta kwa ta oyo
isi na waya oyo
afo na riya oyo
oyo yo oyo
oyo kamba deje kamba
east, west …
– Igbo clapping game

Beatrice

Chubuike is darker than the darkening evening. Bottle-smooth ebony skin. Next to Ivan, another Bangladeshi boy, he is a shadow bouncing around the gymnasium. They are speaking a pidgin mix of English and Igbo, while Simi and I play a clapping game called 'oyo yo oyo' with two other girls.

East, west, north and south, ibidaragay north and south …

We are waiting for the grown-ups to be done with their badminton game so we can play ourselves. When Ivan's father strolls off the court, Chubuike singsongs a greeting.

'Good evening, sah!'

'Good evening, Justice. How are you?'

'I am doing well, sah, thank you.'

Chubuike's Christian name must be Justice. I like Chubuike better. I am surprised he knows English. He doesn't go to our school, so I thought he was a village boy or visiting from another city. Maybe he goes to the boys-only school outside town that Ivan attends, but I can't ask. He's older and male and an outsider and good-looking, each of which alone would have been enough to cut me off, but all together make speaking to him inconceivable.

Ivan turns to us, 'We ah going to split de court and practice, okay? You and Simi take de left side.'

I adjust my hated new glasses and run onto the court. I have argued futilely with my parents that I don't need them, but they are insistent that I do, and are vigilant in not letting me out of the house without them on. This morning, Amma sat me down and pointed to the mango trees to the left of our garage.

'Do you see our oldest tree? Do you see its leaves?' she asks. She's wearing a blue chiffon sari and smells like Oil of Olay.

'Yes,' I say, impatient because I know this is going to be a lecture.

'If you didn't have your glasses, you wouldn't be able to see each leaf, how the wind slips through them, making them tremble.'

But I know that the leaves are there. Do I need to see their shape, their very veins? Why did Simi have to get both perfect eyesight and the dimpled laugh? I am glad only for my darker skin, even though all the Bangladeshis and Indians coo over Simi's butter-honey skin. I have little patience for this particular South Asian prejudice. My inner eye for beauty resolves with the dark.

The gymnasium in Nsukka has the tallest ceilings I've ever seen. Sometimes I imagine there could be clouds above the distant and rusting light fixtures. Chubuike is on my side of the badminton net, alternating lobbing and smashing the shuttlecock at Ivan. Simi and I are practising more conservatively, volleying back and forth, but there's a reason Ivan lets us play with him every evening after school, even though he's a teenager and we're barely into double digits. We've been playing tennis and badminton from the time we could hold rackets, so we're both solid players and can hold our own.

When we start playing for points, I am glad to be on Chubuike's team. He's a little harder to play with than Ivan because he's erratic, but he's fun to watch. He also doesn't get angry the way Ivan does when someone does something wrong. At the end of the game, though we have lost, he turns to me and smiles his limpid vivid smile.

'Good, nneh,' he says. 'Good.'

The next few days open and close, dim with dust. Each time I get home, I slather Vaseline on my lips and take my pinafore to the back porch to shake it out. The leaves on the banana trees look dead, covered as they are with dust. The vegetable garden is faded. As I snap my uniform in the wind, there is little to distinguish the particles flying off the fabric from those in the air. But there's no time to waste. I hang up my uniform, and blink all the way to the gymnasium.

At the gym, Chubuike is restless and distracted. The sky has been heavy the entire day, but still no rain has come. We play a half-hearted game of badminton before we are ousted by a raucous group of university students.

Outside the gymnasium, the air is cool, and Ivan and Simi slip into the tiny public library at the back of the building. My mother's white Peugeot is parked outside, over some flattened weeds. The University of Nigeria has allotted a tiny room for a children's library at the back of the gymnasium, big enough to hold a few hundred books and half-a-dozen people at a

time. The books have been donated by American libraries,
thanks to families in Nsukka with ties to the US. My mother
is helping manage the new library's collection. The American
heroines, Nancy Drew and Judy Blume, have added to my
British Enid Blyton addictions. I wonder if there's been a new
shipment.

Chubuike stands beside me in front of the gymnasium, and
we watch the clouds come together, like a pall falling. He jumps
down the stairs and starts down a path that leads towards the
children's playground. I follow him. The path is so twisted and
overgrown that by the time we reach, no one can see us, though
we're not far away. At the entrance, he turns and looks at me,
then pushes open the little gate and goes inside. I hesitate at a
crackle of thunder, then enter as well.

The children's playground has a slide, some swings, a sand
box, a small jungle gym and a roundabout. Chubuike is scaling
the jungle gym. I put one foot on the roundabout and start
spinning it with my other foot, holding a bright cold metal bar
with one hand. The wind whips my hair around my head, and
I close my eyes, enjoying the lurching inside my body.

Lightning flashes through my eyelids. The roundabout dips
heavily, and I open my eyes. Chubuike is standing in the centre,
balancing as we spin.

'I am leaving,' he says to me in Igbo.

I look at him, bereft but too shy to say anything out loud,
in Igbo or English.

He continues in the forceful rhythmic dialect, 'I know a
word of eight letters. If you divide it, half will make you happy.
Half will make you cry.'

I cannot take my eyes off his face, his red and mobile tongue.
His body surfs the motion of the roundabout. It's slowing and I

give the hard earth another kick to keep it spinning. He wavers and catches his balance by spreading his thin muscled arms.

He switches to English, the slow deliberate way we all speak. 'I give you dis wod, dis name of eight lettahs … Beatrice.'

He gets off the roundabout and leaps over the gate, dissolving into the damp. The rain comes just then, huge chilling drops of water. Puffs of red dust pounce upward with each stabbing raindrop. Within minutes, the drops coalesce into sheets, like being under a waterfall. I spin ever more slowly into the storm.

the last gloaming, 85°F
beans and cassava, fruit and plantain
gari and egusi, maize and sugarcane
run through the grass, past the kola nut trees
across the village chief's huts, his farms and his fields

On Growing

We're standing on the edge of an overgrown clearing. It has come along quite suddenly after a half-hour walk from school. A wild banana tree and some old mango trees list towards the sun. My school has recently added Agriculture to the curriculum, and Form 2X's (grade 8) first assignment begins today.

We file sweatily and alphabetically into an uncertain line and start clearing the field, south to north. This means hacking at stubborn weeds with hoes and machetes, and pulling up rough patches of grass by hand. I am using our family gardener's brand new hoe, its metal blade curved and whole. The handle is a smooth, light-coloured wood, but I can feel my hands getting sore each time I shift my grip.

We're growing corn this season for 'Ah-Greek!' as we call it. In the pocket of my grey pinafore, I have dry yellow corn kernels wrapped in a knot of cellophane. I want to touch the plastic, feel the hard rounded nubs, as I have been doing all day, but my hands are now dirty and damp. My school uniform gets washed once a week, so I have to keep it as clean as I can until the weekend.

Three hacks into my long and narrow row, I discover a tree stump of an unknown species pushing aside the weeds.

'Nneka!' I call. 'Look!'

She is two rows away, progressing with far more ease. I tell myself it's because she's taller. She's got a longer swing with her machete. She leans over to look and laughs.

'Wot fo dis …' I mutter. The pidgin dialect we sometimes use belies our Queen's English command of the language and it lets me feel like I'm blending. I set down my hoe and look around for our teacher, but he seems to have left after his initial instructions.

'Onyocha, lisoon …' Liam says.

I look up, surprised. His calling me 'onyocha,' the standard gibe at foreigners, is unexpected given he is half foreign himself.

He pushes back his dark-gold hair and continues, 'Eez less fo you to cleya. You de be complaining?'

When we heard earlier that we would be allowed off the school compound, our class was overjoyed. But this is turning out to be hard work. The real hoeing, turning the soil and breaking it up into loose clumps won't begin until we've uncovered the ground itself. Liam is right. This means less work for me. I turn back to my plot.

The field where we are planting our corn rows is a short walk from my house. The class has been put at the end of our school day so that we can just go home afterwards instead of going all the way back to school again. When I finally get home, Simi and a Bangladeshi family friend, Shook, are waiting for me in our veranda. They are in grade six at the primary school, which lets out before the secondary school. Shook is still wearing his uniform, his blue and white chequered shirt no longer as crisp as it must have been in the morning. Simi has changed into a sleeveless yellow sundress my mother sewed for her last weekend.

Maher leans into the netted front door, wanting to join us. He's just six and too young to come, but I hug him to my damp body and tickle him to make him laugh.

'Let's go!' Shook says, jumping down the red steps outside our front door. Simi waits long enough for me to drop my water bottle and bag on the floor of our veranda and follow.

'Fasta!'

'One!'

'Two!'

'Tereh!'

We're running as fast as we can. Shook is 'One,' I'm 'Two,' and Simi is 'Three.' Our game is to keep moving, in order. 'One' in front, 'Two' second, and 'Three' third. And we shout our titles every so often. There's no other goal. We have to keep running until we can't run any more. Last time, we played near Shook's house, through a field of maize. Today, we start in the huge cement gutter outside our house. The gutter's bottom is caked with mud and leaves and it narrows in the distance, disappearing into the bush.

A brown speckled lizard scurries before me and I stop short, snagging the tip of my leather sandals on the ground. I barely catch my balance when Simi slams into my back. She grabs my pinafore as we fall together on the red ground. The path has smooth and deep rivulets gouged into it. They look as if they have been there for years, but they were probably carved out by the last rainy season. As I get to my feet, I notice a charcoal cloud hanging to the right, moving away from the bush into the air. There's something burning ahead.

'Shook!' I shout. 'Fa-ya! Stop!'

A village family is setting fire to a section of the fields. After the fire dies out, it will be easy to pace through the burnt grass and pick out the roasted lizards and grasshoppers. And the space will have been cleared for planting.

'We can come back dis way if we ah hongry,' Shook is grinning his gap-toothed smile. He has run back and is waiting for us. His straight black hair is tousled, catching the late afternoon sunlight in loose waves.

'Ugh!' Simi and I exclaim in unison.

Now I am 'One,' Shook is 'Two,' and Simi is 'Three.' We race down a smaller path, away from the fire, holding back the prickly weeds, jumping over stumps and roots. Dust hovers in the air, dulling our skin and clothes. So much for trying to keep my uniform clean.

We emerge into the north side of a small clearing with three mud huts in the centre. This is farther than we've come before. A man wearing a multi-coloured agbada is sitting on a small woven seat outside the largest hut. The ground in the clearing has been recently swept, the broom marks clear. There are two small bowls on the ground. We have interrupted the man's dinner. He stops eating and looks up at us. He will know instantly that we are foreign, our brown skin pale against his, our hair weak in the wind.

He stands up and I notice a machete at his feet. Is he the chief of a small village? How is there even a village here if the university owns all the land in the town? Have we somehow gone beyond the town borders? Doesn't the wall go all the way around? I look around to see if there are more huts hidden in the tall palm trees. Simi is backing out of the clearing. We know we're not supposed to be there. The stories I have heard about juju men, the witch doctors and their spells crystallize in my head. I turn and run back towards the fading light.

The next few calls are whispered 'One ...'

'Shhhh ...'

'Two ...'

'Tereh ...'

The sun is about to set and the crickets are deafening. We have paused, our way uncertain in the encroaching darkness. There are multiple paths to choose from, and though the jungle seems infinite when we're inside, it's usually not difficult to find the way back. But our scare with the village chief has unsettled us.

Simi is tired and crouches on the trail. Her dress flares out around her, a puddle of honey in the looming shadows. Within seconds, an explosion of furious activity commences beneath her dress. To her misfortune, she has settled above a soldier anthill. Soldier ants are bigger than regular ants: head, thorax, and abdomen vividly on display like an anatomical drawing. Their bites are swift and painful. Simi screams and flails while Shook tries to brush off the ants without angering them further. He drags her off the path into the grass, hoping to lose the gleaming black trail streaming out of the anthill. I have to find our way home fast.

We start running again, Simi faltering behind me, and Shook bringing up the rear. I keep the sun at my back and follow the tips of our shadows like arrows. Zig-zagging, we finally emerge into the gorge outside our house. Simi's legs are badly swollen. She scrambles out crying and runs into the house. Shook gets on his bike and rides away.

I climb out more slowly, kick off my sandals, and stand in my favourite part of our compound, the south-west corner, barren of flowers or trees. I'm not worried about Simi. It's true

I've never had so many soldier ant bites at once before, but I don't think you can die from them. And both our parents are home, so they can help her.

Our house is the last one on Ako Okweli Street. The road ends before it reaches us, and the last 100 feet are hard packed dirt. So the west is unobstructed by any man-made objects and a relentless mass of green fills the space before the hills meet the sky. I take off my glasses, wipe them on my pinafore, and look again, for once glad for clear sight.

The horizon is as wide as I can see and the sky violent with the efforts of the sun. The ground is hot from the afternoon and I burrow my feet under the rough red sand to escape the burning.

Next year, our family is leaving Nigeria. The civilian government came to an end two years ago and even the civilians were relieved because there was so much corruption under President Shagari. Now, yet another military coup has occurred and the university has shut down in protest. My father is home, frustrated. His students languish, unable to take their exams or graduate on time.

It has become harder to find fresh bread, milk, or eggs. The stores and markets outside town where we get our groceries – whatever we don't grow in our vegetable garden in the backyard or pick from our fruit trees – have empty shelves or close their doors and stalls early.

Once there was even a curfew. It felt like being in a storybook, even though for the most part, the silence of the curfew was the same silence of the evening, broken only by birdcalls and crickets. Especially since our house is on the edge of town, even quieter than usual.

I had always thought I would go abroad for university on

my own, but now we are going to leave earlier and all together. Either way, it feels too soon and I don't know what to think, let alone how to feel. Plus, we don't even know where we'll end up. The choices are poles apart: Bangladesh, Papua New Guinea, Oman, Tampa, and Pittsburgh. I do know that whichever it is, it could not possibly be this close to the sky.

The sand is almost too hot to bear and the mosquitoes are starting to attack, but I can't leave now. If I can just memorize this sky, by standing here every day, at the edge of the jungle, then it won't matter where I go. Maybe it won't even matter if I never come back. I slap at my arms and legs, and I keep watching.

My mother comes out of the house and calls out to me. She is walking down the steps leading out of the veranda, holding a fragile-looking graft.

'Where did you go that your sister was bitten like that?' she asks me as she bends down to plant the graft.

'Nowheyah, Amma, jost inside de boosh. She did not look fo wheyah she was sitting ...' I protest, forgetting to speak properly in front of her. Before she notices, I point to the scrawny plant in her hand. 'Wot eez dat?'

She smiles, 'It's an orange rose. It has come from Zaria.'

Zaria is in the north of Nigeria, several hundred miles away, in nomad tribe country. We have friends who live there. They must have sent Amma this plant somehow through other friends travelling this way. I watch as she steadies the stem and pushes the earth in around its base.

She continues, 'No one in Nsukka has anything like it.'

I squat down beside her to look at the graft. 'Why ah you planting eet now? Eet's almost dahk.'

'I just got it. I could not wait.' She straightens one of the leaves in the gloaming. The thorns on the stem are sparse but long and sharp, curved and tapered, like claws. I press my finger on the tip of one. It gives, just a little.

'Come in,' she says. 'Wash your hands and face. It's time for dinner.'

I pull open the netted door of the veranda and follow her inside.

My own gardening adventure is starting to absorb me. It takes me two weeks to mould my plot into a loosely-tilled hump. Then I'm ready to plant. I scoop out little holes twelve inches apart and place my kernels in them. The hard work is done, but I'm hooked. Every day I bring as large a jerry can of water as I can carry with me to the field and eagerly examine the warm damp earth for a sign. I am never alone. All my classmates are equally intrigued by their efforts. My plot is among the last to sprout, but it does, finally. And within a week, the straggling shoots are sturdy and a vibrant green. The leaves are so fresh, they look wet and I cannot keep my hands from tracing the veins as I search for dry earth to water.

The orange rose in my mother's garden is not faring as well as my corn stalks. It's growing, but its spindly length is overwhelmed by the white rose climber beside it with its hundreds of tiny white blossoms. And in the corner, as if in defiance, the peach frangipani tree floats an intoxicating scent across our garden, the ground below its knotted branches matted with crushed petals. Every time the orange rose plant sprouts a bud, insects attack. Amma, and soon our whole family, are on a watchful vigil.

'The rose, the rose!' my mother shouts into the veranda where I am playing oga with Simi.

I snatch a broomstick from the broom and leap down the

stairs. There is a fuzzy green striped caterpillar sitting heavily on the rose plant, inches from the precious bud. I know why my mother called me instead of taking care of the prey like she usually does. She has an absurd fear of caterpillars, though no other insect gives her pause. This one is likely poisonous, as pretty as it is. I flick it off with the broomstick, careful not to injure the rose stem. The caterpillar lands on the ground and curls up. I poke it gently with the stick until it half wraps around the tip and I carry it out of the compound.

The next morning, we find a sleek black-and-yellow grasshopper halfway through eating the bud. Simi and I take turns crushing grasshoppers and flicking off beetles. A spray bottle of medicine sits by the front door, and we watch, and we water, and we wait.

Our attendance finally pays off. A month of small tragedies later, a blossom unfolds. As promised, it's orange, radiant amidst the white roses and the pale yellow allamanda flowers. The bloom grows huge and almost droops with its weight. The orange is swirled with fiery red in the centre and fades to lemon on the edges of its petals. Its scent is faint but we bury our faces in its rich insides and breathe deep.

Later that week, an Indian family, the Chaudhurys, come to visit. I wave to them from the corner of the compound where I'm playing hopscotch. They join my parents pacing the veranda. I can hear Abbu talking, ever the professor, with his particular diction and impassioned voice.

'When I was a student at Dhaka University in 1952, I was part of the uprising ...' he is saying.

He's telling Dr Chaudhury about the birth of the Bangla Language Movement in then East Pakistan. About his pride in what Bangladesh accomplished in its war of independence which came almost twenty years after his own march of history.

I am hardly aware of any of this. It's like a game, visiting Bangladesh, even though my family speaks Bangla at home in Nigeria and we eat Bangladeshi food every night. When the Nigerians ask me where I'm from, I say Bangladesh. The country's passport is the only one I hold. We visit almost every summer, and my siblings and I run wild with our cousins, jump in the pond, get fussed over by innumerable relatives, feast like kings, get bitten by mosquitoes, and suffer dysentery of some sort. Then we come home, to Nigeria.

Mrs Chaudhury and my mother are walking in the garden.

'What a lovely colour!' Mrs Chaudhury exclaims to my mother about our pride of an orange rose.

I hop onto a square and look towards them, listening.

'The plant came from Zaria. We have friends we met in Tripoli who live there now. They sent us a graft to grow, but it has given us such headaches.' Amma starts to tell her our little garden saga.

But Mrs Chaudhury isn't paying attention. She reaches out to the rose and snaps off the blossom. I am balanced on a bare foot, clutching a pebble tightly in one hand, open-mouthed.

Oblivious to my mother's still face, she turns and calls to her husband, 'Look! It matches my sari so nicely. Take a photograph!'

My corn plants are higher than my head now. For a moment, I remember to be glad for the abundance, sorry for the frailty and only-ness of my mother's orange rose. I stand in the middle of our cornfield and the forest around me disappears. I am canopied by the leaves and the sunlight and the sky.

bow echo, 73°F

University Hospitals

DISCHARGE DIAGNOSIS AND
INSTRUCTIONS FOR FOLLOW-
UP CARE (physician to complete)

Atypical Depression

PAXIL (Paroxetine HCl)
20 mg Tablet

Uses: This medication is
an antidepressant used
to treat depression.

Side Effects: Stomach
upset, nausea, dizziness,
headache and blurred vision, dry
mouth, constipation, diarrhea,
appetite changes, tiredness, tremor,
nervousness, anxiety, change in sex
drive or sexual ability, sweating,
altered tastes.

**Psychiatric Medical Care Unit
Patient Behavior Guidelines**

Some things that are inappropriate are:
* Going off unit without the proper
  attire
* Focusing on other patient's situations/
  concerns is inappropriate. You are here
  to work on YOU only.

10.06 a.m.

She tells the attending
psychiatrist about the
match castles. For months,
she stood on the fire escape in the bitterest of weathers, and lit
matches. She'd let them burn down to her fingers and place
them in a growing pile. She made little piles of differing
numbers and heights. Somehow, she knew when it was time
to start a new castle.

The psychiatrist doesn't respond to her revelations. She
doesn't know yet that this is how psychiatrists are. And besides,
what did she expect? That he'd understand about the match
castles? That he'd know about the voices as well? The ones in
her head?

She needs to find a good therapist. Someone to talk to and see why she's so tense. So ready to fall.

> I was on the fire escape
> climbing out of drunk
> falling into sober
>
> I think of all the years
> I will spend in this wearying now
> and my heart drops into hell
>
> This is the night again
> and this is my brain on darkness
> Another lonely summer looms

> Silence is a horrible
> spokesperson.

The Home of the Brave

you must begin by vanishing

—Cecily Parks

I have these voices in my head
(put that little girl to bed)
Adult smiling, adult calm
(oh she'll never come to harm)

African Secrets

My thirteenth year has spilt into another dimension. It seems unreal that a few months ago, I was in Nigeria, in a place I understood, even if I didn't belong. Now, I'm on another planet. Public school in Pittsburgh.

There are parts of this year that I can't remember. It's not that blurred together sort of blankness, but more like cauterized memories in which the new and the different are so horrifying and difficult that I can't or won't retain the details. I walk down the school hallways in my stiff new Sears jeans, button-down shirts, argyle sweater vests, and white sneakers. Streams of students, their nasal accents assaulting my ears, flood the school. The snow is like grey rice falling and the sky, what little I can see between the towering buildings, presses down with steely determination.

Simi and I are enrolled in a different school than Maher because he's only in grade one. Every morning, we stand at the traffic signal in front of our house and wait for it to change so we can cross the street and go to school. Fifth Avenue is one of the busiest streets in Pittsburgh. Until late at night, the cars never stop rushing by. I don't dare take my eyes off the light because as soon as it turns, we have to cross, and quickly. It's like being in a giant machine, one that doesn't care if you're slow or afraid or ignorant.

I'm not the slowest or fastest, but I'm always picked last in gym class. I don't know enough about the system yet to know that this isn't good. I can hear the whispers though, and I know that they're about me. As the weeks pass, it's beginning to dawn on me that something about me is drawing attention. But there are so many things I don't understand, it's unclear what it is that's not fitting in.

Perhaps it's my body hair, which I am ashamed of, and so I wear long sleeves and pants every day, no matter the weather. My accent is a slow careful Nigerian version of British English and the subject of much mimicry. My vocabulary is accurate and abundant as per a childhood spent voraciously reading.

I forget both pidgin and the Queen's English in a heartbeat and all my efforts converge on escaping notice at all costs. The first and fastest casualty is my accent. Within six months, almost no one will be able to tell that I didn't grow up in middle America, going to summer camp, and watching bubblegum TV. More gradually, I transform my speech into the slang that I hear my classmates speaking. 'Excellent' becomes 'awesome,' 'vivid' turns into 'hot,' 'clever' into 'cool,' and of course, 'figuratively' is 'like.'

Our school has a gifted and talented education programme with special classes every Monday at another school. You have to score 130 points on an IQ test to attend. The room in which I take the test is smaller than the regular classrooms and there is one other student with me. The test is incomprehensible. Strange shapes I'm supposed to name or describe. Problems whose setting is alien, whose logic I cannot follow. Word play.

Nothing like the Nigerian tests I've taken all my life where boundaries were delimited by teachers and textbooks.

I score a 128 on the IQ test and don't get into GATE. My parents are shocked when I bring my results home. They don't believe me when I tell them the test was difficult, that I didn't understand most of the questions, that I resorted to – of all things – guessing. This isn't like their academically gifted firstborn who has never failed to achieve anything in school before, especially since Simi cleared the cut off by two whole points.

To my horror, they march me to the principal's office and make their case. The IQ test must not have accurately evaluated my abilities. Did the principal know I had never scored less than 95 per cent in any subject? Was he aware I had completed nine years in one of the best schools in Nigeria? That I had come first in every class since fourth grade? In their particular eloquent English, they persuade him that there must have been a mistake. I am enrolled in GATE the next day.

Unfortunately for my parents' efforts, my GATE class involves programming a simple computer game in BASIC. I have never seen a computer before, let alone programmed one. The only time I've seen a keyboard before was in an ill-fated typing class in Nigeria. My classmates and I had to trek to the university where there was a room of typewriters.

We had been warned ahead of time that there would be no chairs in this classroom, so we took our own chairs, balancing the seats on our heads, four chair legs in the sky. Lining up, our wooden caterpillar with human legs had marched its way to the university.

When we got to the typewriting room, we found there was no paper. This was no surprise since there was a chronic paper shortage in town. My classmates and I clacked away at the keys as the hammers hit the empty rolls. The 'return' key was my favourite as such a small keystroke resulted in a sweeping arc of the carriage. Rather than being diminished by the lack of output, my enthusiasm was encouraged by the lack of accountability.

My GATE programming class terrifies me. Why can't we study music like Simi's GATE class? Not that I have any musical talent I know of, but at least I know vaguely how musical instruments work.

With no understanding of what a computer does, I do something I have never done before. I skip class. The second floor bathroom proves a good hiding place after homeroom, and it isn't the only one. The proportion of indoor to outdoor space is yet another point of difference between my life in Nsukka and here. In my Pittsburgh school alone, there are rooms upon rooms in building after building. I feel as if I could walk forever between walls, under roofs and never find the way out. Each Monday, I wait in one bathroom or another until the bus for the GATE programme drives away and then waltz into my regular classes pretending I've accidentally missed the bus.

It doesn't get easier. People hiss cryptic words at me in the hallways: *Ban! African! Secret!*

My gym teacher calls me aside after class one day and asks me if I use deodorant. I am mystified by this question, embarrassed without knowing why. I shake my head. She tells me to ask my mother for some.

I'm not sure what deodorant is, or what it does, but as the hallway remarks continue, including the enlightening *Smelly African!* I eventually link body odour to deodorant. Until now, body odour hasn't occurred to me. The one time it came up was with a maid in Nigeria, who was filling in for our regular maid who had gone to her village to give birth. The new maid apparently smelled. My mother once asked her to take a bath before coming. I recall being puzzled by my mother's request because although I perceived a smell, if I thought about it, I didn't think of it as unpleasant.

It takes me some time to gear up the nerve to ask my parents for money for deodorant. It's not only embarrassment holding me back. I find it difficult to ask for anything that costs money. Since we moved to America, it hasn't been easy for my family. My father was a full professor of geology in Nigeria with generous benefits. Unable to find a tenured position in America easily, he has settled for a private consulting position in a geological firm. My mother used to teach economics in secondary school and is back in school to re-certify herself to teach in a new country. The five of us live in a tiny two-bedroom apartment with rusty appliances and second-hand furniture.

Because there's so little space, it somehow feels like there's not enough time either. We are all learning a new game, an American game, each in our own way. My father is commuting an hour each way to his new consulting job, no longer a few minutes' drive from his office on campus, with doctoral students to advise, syllabi to design, and papers to write. My mother is balancing course work, housework, making three meals a day for a family of five, and taking care of a teenager, an adolescent, and a first-grader.

I am entering my sullen teenage years. I can feel it coming over me as certainly as the clouded sky dome above. My sister, cheerful by nature, is making more friends than I am, but the taunts about our speech and our unfashionable clothes are as difficult to bear, especially since she can't mimic accents as easily as I do. Only my brother, happy-go-lucky baby of the family, appears to be taking the transition in his stride.

Additionally, there is some confusion about how much of this American life Simi, Maher, and I are allowed to absorb. We only eat Bangladeshi food at home. We attend Islamic school on Sundays. We aren't allowed sleepovers or given allowances. So what clothes can we afford that might be cool and still modest? What slang do we adopt that won't offend our parents? What slacker work habits can we get away with? Of course, maintaining high grades is never in question, but patience, which was never plentiful in my overachieving family, becomes even more of a rare commodity.

One evening, I go to the kitchen where Amma is cooking dinner. Maher is near the dining table bumping toy cars into each other. He regroups his cars at my feet. I touch my right heel to my left toes to make a zig-zag obstacle course for him.

I ask, 'Amma, can I have some deodorant?'

She's paying more attention to the chicken korma than to me and asks, 'Why?'

Maher is rolling a red Mustang up my ankle. I struggle not to twitch.

I say, 'Maybe I need some.'

She glances at me and says peremptorily, 'You don't.'

I can tell this is the end of the conversation and leave the kitchen without warning. Maher's protest follows me into the bedroom, but I shut the door.

My walks down the heated and crowded hallways are even more of a nightmare, now that I have labelled my dysfunction. I keep my arms tightly against my sides, dreading the giggles and whispers.

My avoidance of the gifted and talented classes doesn't go unnoticed for long. Confronted by my furious parents, I shakily tell them the truth. The bulky electronic boxes lined up on long tables, the flickering screen, that tiny blinking square cursor waiting for me to do something. I can't do it. I don't know the first thing about how to start.

The last thing I expect is sympathy so I'm astounded to get it. My parents enroll me, and Simi for good measure, in an after-school computer class with rows of neat white Apple IICs, and assignments to print banners, change fonts, and learn typing.

Here again, I stumble. Every action with the Apple computers is mouse-driven, and the mouse I'm supposed to use to control everything sits on the right side of the keyboard. I am left-handed. Not for a moment do I think to shift the flattened sphere and pad to the other side. Nine years of authoritarian Nigerian education and a malleable manner have ensured that I don't question anything, that I make do with what I have.

Not for nothing was I Mr Eze's best pupil, Mrs Okonkwor's little scientist, even the dreaded Mr Chukwuma's French star. I didn't just memorize Blake and Byron, ace arithmetic and algebra, hand in horticulture and history assignments on time and on the mark. I did it all without making a sound.

The act of positioning the cursor, holding it steady while I click and drag, releasing it at the right time and place, all with my non-dominant hand, proves a feat of concentration and effort. Nigh impossible. For weeks, months, I highlight the wrong menu items, I open dialogue boxes I didn't mean to, and I am always last to hand in my work.

Halfway through this first terrible year, my body odour fears

are so intolerable that I return to my mother and insist that I
need deodorant. This time she doesn't protest and I am finally
odourless. One less piece in the endless jigsaw of differences
to set me apart.

By the end of the year, I think I've succeeded in blending
into the background. I get some of the jokes now, but I laugh
behind my hands, in case I'm wrong.

On the last day of my first year in America, I'm in
homeroom, and people are exchanging class photos with their
friends, with silly send-off rhymes written on the back. I have
no photos. They would have been far too expensive, so I didn't
even bother asking my parents about them. Anyway, I have
made absolutely no friends this year. Even the two friends I
used to write to in Nigeria, Nneka and Matu, have drifted away,
the transatlantic postal system too slow or unstable to support
our communications.

Our homeroom teacher is sitting on the edge of his desk,
joking with some students. I still haven't gotten used to the
easy manner in which teachers engage with students here. Just
the fact that he's sitting on his desk, legs splayed, instead of
sternly in his chair, marks a sea change between my classes in
Nsukka and here. Let alone the students bantering, brazenly
questioning.

I'm sitting quietly at the front of the class when a gregarious
classmate calls out to me. I'm startled that he knows my name,
both fearing and anticipating his attention.

'Yeah?' I say with as much American nonchalance as I can
muster.

He says, 'Can I have your picture to smell and remember
you by?'

With this too, it doesn't occur to me to do anything other

than accept what comes my way. I laugh along with everyone else. It's all to be endured and, with effort, understood. I don't speak much that year. It's enough watching my strange new world whirl by.

virga, 51°F

not all of us can gather in
our insides and spill out
the same same
every time
you could call it
being a chameleon
but I'm not
it was the way I learnt to survive in America

Chameleon Girl

I've made a calculated decision to join the swimming team even though I've never been good at sports. After some research, I've discovered that the swimming team in my high school has no try-outs, and the coach, despite being a terror, hasn't been known to cut anyone from her team, ever.

My athletic efforts were futile in Nigeria. The slowest, most ponderous Nigerian girl in school would leave me in her dust. My parents didn't mind my lack of talent in this department. Athletics wasn't as important as other things, like education or religion. Thus, my decision to swim becomes the new cornerstone of our escalating battles for the organization of my life.

'What about your studies?' Abbu asks.

He's concerned enough to put down the latest issue of *Newsweek*. A porcelain lamp beside him sits on a lace doily, two of the few decorative items that made it from our house

74

in Nigeria to here. I'm standing across from him, in front of the curio in the living room. It contains more knick-knacks, most of these from other countries we've visited over the years. Because we were warned not to take any Nigerian art items with us for fear of being accused of stealing artefacts, we have ended up with almost no physical evidence of our time there.

My other sorrow is the decimation of my book collection. When we left, our parents told us we could each take ten books with us. I was devastated. Our library at home was one of my greatest pleasures. Simi, who was not as much of a bookworm, had no trouble selecting her ten. Even Maher spent more time collecting his stash than her. I mourned for weeks. Of course, I had no idea public libraries in America were such a tremendous thing. During my first trip to Carnegie Library in Pittsburgh, I was awestruck, weak with joy. Yet, it doesn't make up for the loss of my old books.

'Swimming is not going to affect my studies!' I tell Abbu with vehemence. 'Anyway, I need a sport when I fill out my college applications next year.'

'You have plenty of other activities. And if it affects your grades, you know what you have to do.' He raises the *Newsweek* back up. The conversation is ominously over.

The trouble with joining the swim team is that I only know the backstroke, and that with no real form, having learnt it in my grandparents' pond in Dhaka when I was a child. It was Babu Mama, my mother's youngest brother, who taught me to swim when I was six. I lay on my back in the dark water, arms stiffly by my side, and he held his hands underneath my back while I kicked. In this way, we got all the way to the middle of the pond, far from all the edges. Then he let go. Even though I knew he was close by, I was terrified. My arms and body rigid, my legs frantic and flailing, I somehow got back to the bank. Even when he shouted that I was close enough to stand up, I didn't dare stop kicking until I could see the edge myself. Only then did I lower my legs through the shallow water into the soft slippery mud.

But it isn't the armless backstroke that we do for four hours a day, six days a week at the high school pool. It's the front crawl, which I have never swum before. I fight through the chlorinated water, laboriously crossing each length over and over again.

At the end of every practice, I avoid the coach's eagle eye, rushing from the humid pool area into the damp locker rooms before she can comment on yet another pitiful performance. Maybe she's never cut anyone, but I am sure that an exception is impending in my case.

Two months into our conditioning, in the middle of another interminable set, I lift my head as usual to take in a desperate breath, and my body suddenly propels through the water with my arm stroke. It's an epiphany. Turning my head just enough to take a breath – instead of lifting my entire head – is not only easier, it's faster. A stretch, a straightening, a twist, a turn, and now, there is power in my motion. Accident, fatigue, or the hundreds of hours of practice have resulted in a smooth front crawl.

I can see the yellow plastic lane lines slide by a little quicker as I swim. Even the length of the pool feels smaller, more manageable. And the locker rooms aren't as lonely. I'm not friends with the other girls in lane six, the slowest lane, the ones with the rookies, the overweight, the small. But we're cordial. We know how much space to give each other as we dive in, one after ungainly other.

I hate swimming but I dream about it all the time.

Despite my new-found breathing skills, I'm still slower than everyone else, and my skin smells chemical. My hair, already unmanageable and frizzy, dries out even more, the ends knotted and split. The culture of counting seconds is consuming, as is shaving before meets, using special shampoos, and ignoring muscle aches and pain.

And I am so afraid of getting cut. I don't try to get friendly with anyone on the team, just in case. How embarrassing it would be to see them at first light, hair wet from morning practices, bodies chlorine-squeaky and strong, complaining about the coach's latest dressing down. I'd have to smile, say hello, and they'd smile back with pity.

Plus, I'm tired all the time. I lose weight even though I eat four huge meals a day and I fall asleep at 9 p.m. every night without doing my homework. What my parents don't know is that the bus ride to school and homeroom has been enough to maintain my grades since we moved to America. The suburban public high school system in Pittsburgh is nothing compared to the rigours of Nigerian education. I ace every exam with minimum effort.

It's good because I can't afford much energy for schoolwork anymore. My body has been so wholly taken up by the difficulty of swimming that it requires my mind. It's taken me until now to understand that a physical pursuit can be as challenging, if not more so, than an intellectual one. It's my first honouring of the body.

'Perhaps you should quit,' Amma says worriedly, hopefully. 'You don't even have the energy to eat sometimes.'

'But my times are getting faster and faster. Not that you'd know from coming to any of my meets.'

Maybe my parents are protesting my baffling athletic

endeavour by boycotting them. I also have the vague thought that the one-piece racing suits we wear are a factor. They are as modest as swimwear gets, but not ideal gear for young Muslim girls. In any case, I'm being unfair. I don't actually want my parents to come to my meets when it's clear I'm just not that good.

'Just keep your grades up. That's what's most important.'

The arguments are more difficult, because I'm not sure if I should keep swimming, even though I like the way my body is changing. My muscles are emerging, thinly, strongly, everywhere. By now, I've spent enough time on the team to pencil in a sport on my college applications. And how healthy can it be to be so tired all the time?

But I don't quit. It's become a matter of pride. This is the hardest thing I have ever done in my life and I don't want to give up. I cannot let my parents detect a shadow of doubt in my words.

Our English class has been assigned to keep a writing journal. The cheap yellow notepad fills up in weeks and is the first of many to go into my nightstand drawer. Finally, I have an outlet for the thoughts I can't express anywhere else. One, in particular, haunts me, and for days no other words get through: '*I can't wait.*' These three words fill page after page in my journal. College. I cannot wait to leave home. I've been ready for years.

Our family has moved out of our tiny two-bedroom city flat into the suburbs. We have a house now, with yellow aluminium siding, three bedrooms, two-and-a-half baths, and a lawn. Our parents, with a stroke of insight, let Simi and me have the master bedroom. It's a bigger room with a double closet, easier to fit two twin beds, but the real coup for teenage girls is the en suite bathroom.

Outside our sunlight-deprived house is a neighbourhood that hasn't yet accepted us, nor have we accepted it. Four years and I've not been inside any other house on our street except our own. Four years and our house is the only one egged on Devil's Night.

When it first happens, we don't even know what Devil's Night is. Of course, we know about Halloween. It's hard not to in America, with the proliferating orange banners, the pumpkins for sale on the roadside, masks and costumes in every store front, all dead giveaways.

Simi and I love the idea of trick or treating, but as teenagers, it feels like we're too old, and Maher is too young to go on his own. Besides, we don't have anything to wear. Making costumes is out of the question. It would be too embarrassing to join the hoards of department store outfitted ghouls and vampires, wearing homemade princess dresses. We haven't been here that long, but we know that much. Buying costumes, on the other hand, is an unwarranted expense.

We settle for handing out candy to costumed children. At the end of October throughout high school, my mother prepares a big bowl full of Jolly Rancher, her favourite, and Kit Kat bars, our favourite. Since the Kit Kat bars are expensive and there aren't as many of them, we are instructed to be judicious in our treating. The trick part of the ritual is mysterious and frightening and we never plan on asking anyone for one of those.

Despite all the preparation, we get tripped up our first crisp Pennsylvania fall. The night before Halloween, a series of sharp cracks sounds outside our living room window. We rush to the window, and instead of armed robbers, we see nothing. This is because egg yolk is coating the outside of the window.

'What is it?' my father yells from the family room.

'Egg!' Maher crows in recognition.

I look at my little brother in annoyance. Why is he so happy? But it's true that Maher is teaching us something, something our stiffly formal family has sore need of learning, especially now, during our uncomfortable assimilation with America. With his ready hugs and easy manner, my baby brother is single-handedly making touching a part of our family's greetings and goodbyes. He complements Simi's clowning, which had existed in isolation until he was old enough to engage. He laughs all the time. And we adore him, this beautiful baby who came so late that even Simi and I could watch him grow up. Even when I have not a shred of goodwill towards anyone else, I have nothing but love for Maher.

'Why would one waste perfectly good eggs by throwing them like this?' Amma asks in puzzlement.

Abbu comes to look. Shaking his head, he says, 'Only a rich country with too much food would think of it.'

Amma turns to practical matters. 'How are we going to clean the outside of this window?'

Our living room is above the garage, on the second floor, a difficult, maybe impossible place to reach. I'm sure I'm going to be volunteered for the task. After an hour of washing and wiping, I venture out with Simi. A furtive rain is falling, vanishing before reaching the ground. Some of the houses on our street sport Halloween decorations, white plastic ghosts hung from the windows, pumpkins on porches. There are trees here and there, dotting the lawns on each property, their sparse shadows only highlighting that there aren't enough of them.

Our reconnaissance reveals no other egged houses in our neighbourhood. But why? After little deliberation, we decide it's because we're brown. Our family is practically the only non-white one in our suburban Pittsburgh township. This incident doesn't offend or scare us as much as annoy us, and every year, the same thing happens. None of it brings us together. I am only more eager to leave.

By my third swim meet, I can swim the 100 free, four lengths of the pool, forty-five seconds faster than when I joined the team. This doesn't get me out of lane six, but it's something. The next day, I find myself heaving as I walk back home from the bus stop. The weather is turning wintry and the fact that I can see my breath in white clouds makes my labouring more obvious. Again, I am assailed by uneasiness. Why am I always so tired? Maybe I *should* quit.

As I walk into the house, the phone rings. It's Todd, my only friend in high school, a red-haired runner who spent numerous lunch periods breaking through my determined silence. Our house has one phone and it's in the kitchen, so private conversations are pretty much out. Todd wants to know if I'd like to go to a movie this weekend. I look over at Amma. She's at the sink, using paper towels to pull the skin off chicken legs. We're having a big dinner party tonight, and the house is filled with the smell of spices. She won't have time to think, which means she'll say no. Then, if I ask the next time, she might be irritated and say no even more firmly. I make a decision.

'Sorry,' I tell him. 'Maybe the weekend after.'

The week ahead will give me some lead time to plan how and when to ask. My parents don't approve of after-school activities that aren't school sanctioned or academic or Bangladeshi or Islamic in nature. But the real problem is that Todd is a boy. We aren't dating. This isn't an option, whether I wanted to or not. Dating is too extreme to consider.

Unfortunately, movie-going is also on the forbidden spectrum, not seemly or practical, let alone with boys.

The operator breaks into Todd's phone call, 'An emergency call needs to be put through.'

I hang up on Todd and take the other call. It's Abbu, calling from work, wondering why the phone was busy. He wants to know if Amma needs anything from the grocery store on his way back from work.

'Who were you talking to for so long?'

'Jessica,' I say immediately, my dissembling skills more honed each year. I think about what classes Jessica and I have together and which subject will hold the most caché with my scientist father. 'We were going over our physics homework …'

'Didn't you see her at school?' he asks, though his tone is mollified. 'You have to talk to her again?'

It's 9 p.m., and I'm wearing a blue silk shalwar kameez that shimmers as I move through the guests. My voice lowers, softens, when I speak to Bangladeshi adults. A child in a tiny red kurta runs underfoot as I offer one of the uncles a soft drink.

The party is a success. Somehow, Amma has managed to cook more than enough food for forty guests, and it all tastes like heaven. The table is laden with biryani, chicken korma, daal, shrimp with squash, catfish, eggplant mash, vegetable stir-fry, sautéed green beans, and a huge fresh salad.

Afterwards, Simi loads the dishwasher and I bring out the desserts: ice cream, home-made pineapple upside-down cake, firni, and a beloved Bangladeshi dessert: sweet dense white balls of roshogolla.

These dinner parties take up most of our weekends. One family or another in the growing community of Bangladeshis in Pittsburgh throws a dinner party pretty much every weekend. And then there are the twice yearly celebrations for Eid, which are even more feastful fancy affairs that sometimes stretch out over several days. The actual day of Eid usually lands on a weekday, and most of the Bangladeshis take at least the morning off from work if possible, to go to the mosque to pray. Those who can, take the day off, unpaid, and go from house to house wearing new clothes and eating up a storm. The weekends become a way for those who couldn't join on the actual day to cook and feed and visit each other.

For our parents' generation, these parties are the only kind of gathering where they can relax and speak Bangla. Our attendance at these events is mandatory and reluctant. There are almost no kids my or Simi's age. Even Maher is years older than everyone else. We don't know how American families spend their weekends, but we'd rather be home reading or watching some forbidden TV. Our only conversations are when we are being interrogated about our academic pursuits in college, and we have all the right answers ready.

'I'll be studying engineering, uncle,' Simi says earnestly.

'Mathematics, aunty,' I say with equal and can-do fortitude.

Only Maher, entering adolescence and too young for college conversations, escapes, for now.

In my senior year of high school, Simi joins the diving team. My parents aren't pleased, but they don't put up as much resistance.

'At least we can pick you up together after your practice ends,' my mother says.

I try not to shrug as exasperation is grounds for a lecture. Despite the fact that we talk easily at home, Simi and I don't speak to each other at school. It's an unspoken understanding. These worlds, school and home, cannot intersect. There are too many hierarchies, of age, social standing, personality, attractiveness, academic ability, sportsmanship, after-school activities, and other dimensions I can't perceive, let alone internalize. And besides, Simi is more outgoing and less benighted by the awkward adolescent years. Her friends are involved in everything, from theatre to prom. I only have Todd.

At 7 a.m., a claustrophobic winter sky looms above. Simi bangs on the bathroom door.

'Hurry up!' she yells.

I emerge, dressed in a black mini skirt and a tight grey blouse.

Amma is calling from downstairs. 'The school bus will be here soon!'

I tug jeans on under my skirt and grab a long black sweater that covers both the blouse and the mini skirt. By the time I put on my winter jacket, my secret outfit is doubly concealed.

The high school bathroom smells sticky sweet and smoky. The prom queen is spraying her three-inch-high bangs higher. Her glossy lips purse as she sprays. Two other girls are arguing as they go through their crammed purses for cigarettes and lighters. I sneak into a toilet stall and unpeel my layers. None of the girls notices me, but I wait for them to leave before I come out of the stall. By the eighth period, I'll be back in disguise.

We have a no-TV-after-8 p.m. rule, so it's quiet in our house at night. Amma and Abbu read downstairs, while Simi and I do our homework and talk in our bedroom until we fall asleep. I look cautiously into the living room. Is it a good time to bring up going to the movies? My parents are sitting in separate puddles of yellow lamplight. Abbu is reading *National Geographic*, rubbing his stomach, yet another of his habits that I've picked up.

There's a childhood story my family tells, in which someone

remarks that I'm like my father. Upon hearing this, I furiously stamp my feet. *No!* I shout, *I don't have a bald spot!* Proving that, at the very least, I have inherited or absorbed Abbu's temper.

'Can you help me with something?' Amma asks, startling me.

I walk over to where she's sitting beside piles of textbooks and paper. Amma is still on her quest to teach again. She has been taking courses at CCAC, the local community college, to get back into the swing of academics. In Nigeria, her subject was economics, but in her quietly adventurous way, she has enrolled in a wide range of classes from computers to mathematics. I've been helping her with her math homework, but looking at her assignment, I realize she's outpaced my progress in high school.

'Sorry, Amma,' I say. 'We haven't learnt that formula yet in trigonometry. Your class is fast!'

'Have you done your homework?' Amma asks, though she sounds distracted.

'Yeah,' I say, even though I haven't started it.

It doesn't seem the right time to ask about a movie, so I go back upstairs. Three days later, I gather up the courage to ask. By this time, I have an army of answers ready, four truths and one lie (who I'll go with):

I'd like to watch a PG-13 movie called Biloxi Blues *at Century III Mall. I'd go with Becky and she'll drive. The movie is an hour and forty-seven minutes and I'll be back in three hours. Yes, I did see a movie already this month, but this one is supposed to be good. Thank you, Amma and Abbu!*

More often, I get an unexplained refusal, or thwarted agreement.

'Abbu, I have to attend the School Spirit dance because I helped organize it as part of the student government.' I'm trying to keep a balance of pleading and firmness in my voice. The rules about dating extend implicitly towards dances and I know I'm on unstable ground.

'You've already organized it. Why do you have to go?'

'I'm helping check the tickets at the door,' I say. This part is true.

'When does it start?'

'Eight.'

'And how long will the ticket selling last?' My father hasn't looked up from his newspaper.

'I don't know …'

He looks up at me and waits.

'Till nine?' I say uncertainly.

'Okay, your mother will pick you up from the school at 9.15.' He looks back down at the paper.

I can't show how sullen I feel, not if I want to go out every so often. The closer it gets to my leaving for college, the less I ask my parents for permission for each prized outing. I have to be so good for so long, ask so nicely, and still be prepared for immediate and likely rejection. It's depressing and humiliating. I'd rather stay home. And once I get to college, I won't have to ask anyone anything.

Still, sometimes I can't help myself, and more often than not, things turns sour.

'Since when do children defy their parents?' Amma and Abbu exclaim, when my angst gets the better of me.

'Since you brought us here, that's when,' I say recklessly, always too quick to anger.

'We can always send you to Bangladesh. You can do college there and it will be far less expensive. And then you can marry a nice Bangladeshi boy.'

There's nothing to say to that. Together, we unfairly and

fairly blame America for our troubles. They turn their backs. I join the ranks.

Our last swimming meet of the season is at Trinity High School. We enter the pool area, swinging our arms like windmills, jumping in place in the hot and humid air. Because there are so few divers, the coaches of the opposing teams decide to hold the diving events halfway through the meet. While the divers perform, the swimmers sit in two rows behind the springboard, the boys against the wall, the girls in front of them.

Simi steps up for her dive, a single backwards somersault. Her hair is cut asymmetrically, the right side a smooth black wave cupping her jaw, the left side close to a buzz cut. Her face is solemn, no sign of her easy dimples.

I hug my knees to my chest, distracted. I have a race coming up that I've never done before, the hundred butterfly. One of our three fly swimmers is sick and so I've been inserted into the line-up. The other team has fielded only two swimmers for this event, so there's an empty lane. This means that even if I come last, I'll still score points for our team. But my goal is just to finish the race.

As the coach has taught us, I visualize. That place before the start. The block's bubbled exterior rough under my feet. One foot behind, the other forward, toes off the block, crouched down, fingers gripping the leading edge. In my mind's eye, I tuck my head, swaying slightly with anticipation, and jack-knife into the blue, the pocket of air under my stomach popping, as I slice into the water.

Simi walks along the springboard to its jouncing end. Facing out, she bounces once and leaps out. But she's not leapt far enough. As she tucks her legs up and arches backwards, the back of her neck comes down on the board, and she falls with a splash into the water.

I am frozen in place, dread crushing my lungs. In the same heartbeat, I feel air rush over my head as the boys' captains leap over my head and launch into the water.

Simi wants to get out of the pool. She's conscious, distressed. The coaches are shouting to the boys from the edge of the pool.

'Hold her up! Don't move her!'

'Stay where you are! Hold her head above water!'

'DON'T LET HER GET OUT!'

My limbs finally unlock and I crawl to the side of the pool. The ambulance comes within minutes and the paramedics lower the stretcher into the thrashing water. Carefully they strap my little sister into the stretcher and only then do they raise her out of the pool.

I follow her stretcher towards the waiting ambulance, barefoot in a racing suit, half-running, watching her bloodless face, unable to think or feel anything.

When she sees me, she says, 'You have to go back. You have to swim your last race. You've never done the hundred butterfly, and it's your last meet, your senior year.'

'Are you crazy? I'm coming with you. Forget the race.'

'No, you have to go back,' she says even more urgently. 'You have to do your last race. Go back.'

I hesitate for a split second. Am I supposed to do what she asks, even though it's absurd? The momentum of the paramedics pushes me aside.

'Do your race!' she calls, as they run her stretcher outside to the waiting ambulance.

I come second in the hundred butterfly. Powered by fear

and a sense of futility, I breathe every other swooping stroke, my arms scissoring the water under my torso in those twin mirroring curves unique to the butterfly. Only the regional champion touches before me.

I spend the next two weeks in the waiting room of the intensive care unit of the hospital with my parents and brother. I am too numb and afraid to feel my heart in my mouth. Is this somehow my fault? Because we stayed up talking almost all night before the meet?

Simi and I spend night after night in imaginary worlds of our making. We have been doing this since we played with Lego dolls and Barbies as children, making up characters and stories for them. At some point, we abandoned the dolls, forced by strict bedtime routines, and moved on to whispering to each other, lying in our parallel beds in the darkness, role playing. True to colonial influence, our characters have prim English names, but live in lush tropical climes. They have what we used to think were unreal eye colours, like purple or gold or green. Growing up, we couldn't imagine eyes that changed with the light or the sky, that blended easily with the grass or the sea.

In the mornings, I wake bleary-eyed, knowing there's all of school to get through, then swimming practice, homework, and chores. I have to wait all of the unforgiving day until the night when we can continue telling each other stories. We even have a code word for it, curly ear, based on a gesture we make to each other when we're with others, a hand curling around an ear, signalling it's time.

You know she's not as strong as you.

I can hear my mother's voice in my head. Is it true? Was it exhaustion that held her back when she jumped from the board? Was it our curly ear addiction? What if she dies? What if she's paralysed? How could I possibly go on normally?

Simi has separated her fifth and sixth vertebrae, those that control motion, but a fraction of a millimetre has saved her from paralysis. She lies strapped to a bed with a metal halo affixed around her head, a length of steel down her spine to keep everything in line.

A few days into her ICU stay, a young French surgeon stabilizes her two separated vertebrae with a metal plate and screws. Instead of stitches, he uses a new kind of bio glue to close up the seven-inch incision along her neck. He tells us about this glue in the bald light of the waiting room, and we let his excitement percolate around us, as if it will hold us up, hold Simi together.

The X-rays show an astounding sight. The delicate bones of her spine interlock invisibly until the injured part, where a rectangular plate sits harshly along two vertebrae. It's as incongruous as a hammer on glass. Fat screws pierce the four corners of the plate, spiralling through into blood and nowhere.

When Simi is released, she wears a hard neck brace for months, a soft one for the rest of the year. She doesn't return to school until her senior year, after I've graduated and gone off to college. They say she might not be able to do competitive sports again, but we care only that she's alive, that she can walk. Even so, the weight I've been feeling all this time, of guilt and responsibility, remains, throbbing anew each time I see her lift her head off the pillow in effort and pain. I can tell that I will never stop feeling it. It makes my desire to leave for college keener, more complicated, less satisfying a dream, and more urgent.

The swimming season is over, along with our gruelling practices, but I'm still out of breath. As I climb to the second floor at school, I catch myself whispering a number. I stop on the landing and look down the stairs. It dawns on me, what I'm doing. I'm counting. Stairs, seconds, steps.

Somewhere in my brain, a clock is going, like the one in the pool room. It never stops. *Faster faster faster.* I'm half-running everywhere all the time, leaving myself no time for rest, because that's how our coach runs each practice. Every stride, every stroke, every motion of my body, in or out of the water, is even and paced.

That's when I realize I'm no longer tired. I'm moving faster, more powerfully, than I used to. I have figured out one thing in my American life, even as everything else feels picked apart. My body feels loose and liquid, my skin sliding easily over muscle and bone.

11.03 a.m.

She is fevered. The rooms revolve in stainless steel and dull white and she is ill with it. She can't stand the throbbing in her head. The air is dry, and the skin on her face feels too tight. If she smiles, she'll crack.

The nurse on desk duty is a brisk no-nonsense woman.

'I want to take a shower,' she tells her.

The nurse waves Wendy over, who trails her to the large damp shower room. The walls are dark and the corners unclear. She showers as Wendy stands in the doorway, waiting and watching. The water feels too wet, her skin too real.

```
     I
   list
    in
    my
  waters
  leaning
     to
    mad
   intent ...
```

11.30 a.m.

Jim sits beside her at the community meeting. He is a patient, large and unkempt, in a kindly sort of way. On her other side, they park a woman in a wheelchair. She hasn't ever seen the woman alert. Her eyes are always half-closed. She wants to catch her aware, like that guy in *Awakenings*, a suddenly piercing stare. Instead, midway through the meeting, the woman lets her bladder loose. She gathers her limbs close around her, as the pale liquid streams under the chairs.

'What are your personal goals?' the meeting leader asks someone.

The answer is ready. 'To get well and go home to my kids.'

The circle moves on and stops at her. She racks her brains. She is twenty-five years old and she can't think of a single personal goal she either has or wants to have.

Finally, driven to speak, she says, 'To find out my personal goals.'

```
                I feel blasé and out of it.
                 I feel sharp and reckless.
                    I feel stupid and slow.
                   Most of all, I'm tired.
                         I'm tired of being.
    Not that I'm working that hard at being.
                      I'm tired of thinking.
         I'm not thinking that much either.
             I'm tired of wearing my face.
```

dog star days, 91°F
glass through a window
lass through a life
she will destroy
what she's given

Burning

I want to kiss Chloe. Ever since I realized that girls are softer than boys, and that soft isn't always bad, I've been wanting. The give of her stomach, the sine curve from breast to waist to hip. I imagine my hand flat against that smooth pale skin below her throat, that most beautiful place in girls.

I've come to the University of Pennsylvania with a promise four years in the making. I'm not the pretty one in the family. Simi is. And I've never known how to be funny. So I'm trying a third tack: I'm going to be bold. Bold in Wharton with all the business honours students, bold in Hill Housing Dining Hall with the dark-haired boy who sits in the far corner with his lacrosse friends, bold in the King's Court dorm lounges with their scratchy chairs and sappy couples. Bold with Chloe.

Chloe is assured, with alabaster skin, an anthro major. She has a small flame of a smile, a blue gaze, and short blonde hair that whips around in the wind.

Her eyes narrow even as she smiles. 'Why do you always come to these LGB parties?'

'I wanted to see you.'

I'm becoming terrible at avoiding questions. All the years

94

of avoidance and dissembling with my parents erode in one fell season. The truth ends up coming out as fast, sometimes before I know what I'm saying, another dangerous game.

She takes my hand and pulls me onto the dance floor. We're in the basement of the Gold Standard, near the Christian Association Centre, the only non-frat party on Thursdays. It's a restaurant by day. Chairs and tables are piled into the corners, and the makeshift spotlights are uneven and blinding. Here, who I am and who I'm with melt away, leaving only the music and the motion.

I don't know where I'm getting my ideas from. Not from my immigrant Bangladeshi Muslim parents or my small-town upbringing in Nigeria. Nor yet from my prom and pop culture Rust Belt high school. Somehow, I'm growing up a flirt.

Will I kiss Chloe? I'm sure I will, during Spring Fling, tipsy on a rum concoction we call love juice. She leans into me, our fingers brushing, and I am overcome by the intimacy, the heat of skin touching, as if by accident. My heart almost pounds out of my chest, her lashes fall, and fuck. Glenn shows up just then on the heels of a downburst. But the rain and love juice fogs all our eyes so nothing seems out of place. I don't see Chloe again for months.

Glenn is Wolfman, and Wolfman is free, even though we've been inseparable since we met at the orientation. I know he still dreams of his high school girlfriend who was a lifeguard, and so I don't begrudge the smell of chlorine in my hair after swimming. The cold bleached smell radiates off my skin as I run back from Gimbel Gym, my breath clouding around my head, silver lining my vision, so I imagine I have a super power. I will have what I want, I will take what I want, and most of all, I will say what I want. I will engage instead of watch, which is what

I've done for the last four years, my first four years in America. I will wield this power of spilling truth to get Glenn with his silly yellow tie and quick wide smile. Glenn of constant motion, life an obstacle course to be jumped over, kicked aside, thrown back. Glenn, my sharp-tongued funny first love.

'All of which are American dreams …' Glenn is singing Rage Against the Machine.

'Which American dreams?' I ask.

'Olive Witch, *I* am your American dream.'

Glenn's twisted lyric hits home and I am breathless with the possibility.

It's not easy speaking, after all the silence, of thinking dangerously, because I knew none of the dangerous thoughts would ever come to light. But I have learnt this much from my years of observation in high school: people don't say what they think. They all talk around the centre, never once stepping into the spotlight where the real thing is dancing, begging you to flail, if you would for a second, with the truth. So I make it my niche. I tell the truth sooner, no matter how alone and exposed it makes me feel.

In the morning, I awaken first, Glenn's arms wrapped around me, his breath warm at the base of my neck. When I disentangle, he reaches for me in his sleep, and I touch his unknowing lips. My stomach growls in hunger and I grab the loaf of bread from the top of the mini fridge. As I drip honey onto the bread, his fingers find my feet, enclosing my toes in his palm. His eyes open, olive and opaque, and just like that, the day registers.

My first two years at Penn are a haze, every experience intimate and disconnected. I have the sensation that my body is so inside the world that the details take over, dispelling all sense of boundaries. The watchful teenager I used to be, the serious child, I blow it up, even though I have nothing to replace it with, only the hunger of touching. Nothing matters except what's under my hands, my skin, the immediate now.

I return to Pittsburgh to spend my second summer of college at home. It's a huge mistake. After all the freedom of university in a big city, inserting myself back into suburban Pittsburgh, into my family, is like reliving my torturous high school years, but worse because I know what's out there.

Every day, at 7.30 a.m., my mother drops me off at the bus station in Elizabeth. The bus rolls through western Pennsylvania suburbia for fifty minutes, past three rivers and hills upon hills, before reaching downtown Pittsburgh. I sleep the entire way, missing the one part of this city I've come to love, the rusted sprawl of industry, factories flaming into the ominous sky, others emitting foul odours despite years of disuse.

My summer job downtown involves data entry, eight hours a day. Many of my co-workers are young black single mothers. They talk about boyfriends, baby daddies, husbands, and exes. This one is in jail, the other even farther, and that one was never close enough to touch. They've skipped the stage I'm in, the part that's all potential, or it was over too fast, long ago. Many of them go to a second job right after this one. At $7 per hour, I don't know how they manage, even with two jobs. My meagre earnings are for school. My bus fare and meals are provided by my parents. I have nothing to say, everything to learn from these women, but there's a gulf between us I don't know how to bridge.

My reading project for much of the summer is an epic 1,000-page book, another point of divergence. My co-workers read glossy magazines, if anything. Ironically, my book, *Roots* by Alex Haley, is telling me their history, a history that's rarely taught in schools. Every day, during our half-hour lunch and two fifteen-minute breaks, I immerse myself in Kunta Kinte's savage story of slavery. Then I go home.

In the evenings, I write to Glenn. Phone use in our house is so restricted and public, I'd rather write letters. Glenn is working as a camp counsellor in central Pennsylvania. It's the first time we've been apart in two years, and I'm wrought with it. Despite my ordinary schedule and smothered lifestyle, I find a million things to write about. From the volume of words I send via post to Carlisle, it must be clear how obsessively I think of him, what he means to me, who I have become in this unit of us. Glenn's weekly letters back are my summer's only delight. His loopy little-girl handwriting and the names he makes up for himself on the corners of the envelopes are instantly recognizable. I savour every word.

One evening, I get another letter. It's from a local Pittsburgh organization that gives out scholarships to university students with African ties. Somehow they've found out about my Nigerian connection and they've awarded me $2000 for college. I am ecstatic. Every year, my family negotiates with Penn's financial aid office to try get more funding, more grants. Despite winning half-a-dozen merit scholarships, and tens of thousands of dollars from both within Penn's grant system and from external sources, it's proving difficult for my family to cope, especially now that Simi has started college. Her school, Johns Hopkins University, is in the state of Maryland, so she's ineligible for the Pennsylvania grants I'm getting as a state resident. We are counting every penny.

I know by now that Nneka and many of my classmates in Nigeria will be enrolled in UNN, the university my father taught at for fourteen years. Or they will have left Nsukka for universities and jobs in Enugu, Ibadan, Jos, Benin, Kano, Zaria, and Lagos, or they will have gone abroad. In another couple of years, even those in Nsukka will have gone. It is a university town, its population bounded by those studying or teaching there.

'You cannot accept this,' Abbu says after reading the letter.

'What do you mean?' I ask, shocked.

'It's not for you. This scholarship is for black students.'

'No, it's for students who have ties to Africa,' I protest.

'They mean blacks. What if you went to their office? What would they think when they saw you? When it was clear that you weren't black?'

I think about Kunta Kinte, his unthinkable trials repeated a million times over the centuries to where America is today.

With less force in my voice, I say, 'But we need the money.'

'They need it more.'

In the break room at work, I read the scholarship offer one last time and then pitch it in the trash with the fast food wrappers and coke cans. I shut my book and take out Glenn's latest letter.

My lovecrush is so overpowering that I don't perceive the tension mounting in our house. So when my father asks why I must write Glenn so often, I'm not as careful as I usually am with my words.

'I like writing to him,' I say, capping and uncapping my inky blue pen as I look out the living room window. 'Nothing seems real until I've told him.'

Outside, the summer heat shimmers on our black tar driveway. I notice the grass has to be cut. Maher is still too young to handle a bulky bladed machine on his own, so it falls to me and Simi to mow the lawn, and we hate it. We have a used lawnmower whose starter is so reluctant that it requires dislocating your shoulder to get going. I don't know why Americans love their sprawling lawns so much. I prefer the British model: chock-full of flowers, like our ever-blooming garden in Nigeria.

'Are you dating this boy?' Abbu asks. Everything he says with that stern face, those full lips, I feel it like an accusation.

'Yes.'

Maher gets up and goes upstairs. My gangly teenage brother is somehow avoiding the hostility that has marked my relationship with my parents since I was his age. He simply disengages. I wonder if our parents' ensuing bewilderment and frustration at his behaviour is better than this, this toxic anger sucking at the air.

'You know that we don't recognize dating in our culture,' Abbu says. 'You must stop at once.'

'But, Abbu, I love him!' I burst out. I do. I'm in hopeless velveteen love with Glenn.

'If you marry him, or someone not of our faith, let alone culture, understand this: you will no longer belong in this house.'

'You would choose religion over your own child?'

'I would.' Abbu starts walking away.

Simi takes this chance to flee the scene. My sister is the gentlest of us all, save Amma. She wants us all to get along and goes to great lengths to avoid disagreement.

I follow Abbu into the family room in desperation. The walls are covered with dark brown wood panelling and hideous family portraits, every marker of 80s adolescence on display: Simi's asymmetrical haircut and wild print tops, and my frizzy hair, braces, and glasses. Only Maher looks cute, poised to skip the fugly years.

'Abbu, if I were to marry Glenn, what would you do?'

'Are you going to marry him?' He doesn't look at me.

'Maybe ... Yes ... I think so.'

'Then this is no longer your home. You will no longer have my name.'

I storm upstairs to my bedroom startling Simi when I fling open the door. She darts out as I start throwing clothes into my backpack. Amma tearfully tries to calm me, as she always does during family fights, but this time I don't listen.

The screen door bangs behind me as I leave the house and walk through Amma's flower plants down the sloping driveway. The roses are constrained to a small central patch on our front lawn. Their slender thorned presence is overwhelmed by the expanse of green on all sides.

I get to the top of the hill at the end of our street and sit down on the sidewalk under a sapling tree, already dripping sweat. The shade is meagre and a truck lumbers past, blowing exhaust and dust in my face. I close my eyes and even though it's laughable, I try to channel Prince Siddhartha sitting under a tree, wisdom burning around his smooth bald head, like rays from the sun.

Where do I go? What could I do? I think back through all the jobs I've had. The data entry job I currently hold. Analysis for a small think tank last summer, most of which time I spent playing Tetris. Research for an economics professor during my sophomore year. A retail sales job at Kids"R"Us. And my first source of independently earned income: working drive-through at the local McDonald's in high school. A wave of panic in my stomach roils up, as I envision doing any of these jobs full-time and permanently.

Then I think about what it means not to have my parents by my side. What comes to mind immediately, the one subject

Abbu and I have always agreed on, what I've been indoctrinated in, is the value of higher education. My parents were both trained as teachers and expect that their children will follow their footsteps into higher education. It's understood that we will end up with PhD's after our names. It doesn't matter that I don't know what I want to do with my life. Uncertainty is not a strong argument in our family. Without their help, I cannot finish college. My Ivy League school costs more than I know. I have to go back.

As if on cue, Amma drives up in her little blue Horizon to where I'm sitting on the curb. She rolls down the window, eyes large and teary. 'Come home. Your father is very upset. He didn't mean to tell you to leave.'

'He said exactly what he meant, Amma.'

'I know it's hard for you to understand him – '

'Well, he's not trying to understand me!' Righteousness rises in my tone, even though moments ago I was ready to capitulate.

'Come home, baba, please.' Her voice trails off.

I can't look at her because I know she's crying. I get into the car.

The silence in my parents' house is claustrophobic. I sit upstairs in my room as the fan pushes the hot air around. I can't write my letters anymore. Instead, I press the pen hard into my journal, watching the ink blot and stain each page. It's as if I'm not real, only acting out a part: a wayward daughter, a conflicted immigrant with ever more tenuous ties to Nigeria, an American in Bangladeshi clothes, a Bangladeshi with American attitude.

A few weeks ago, our family went to the Pittsburgh courthouse, and we renounced our Bangladeshi citizenships, swore oaths to America. Only Maher didn't have to go because he's a natural-born citizen. It felt like nothing to me, neither

America nor Bangladesh the country of my heart, but both more tangibly tied and now untied to my identity.

When I return to Penn for my junior year, the trickster autumn matches my mood, reckless, restless, pointless. There's an Asian dancer-activist who's been around campus for years. This season, she's wearing an outrageous outfit: little American flags in the shape of round pasties, stuck on her flat chest, and an impossibly small bikini bottom. It's chilly, and I wonder if she's cold. She's oh-so-thin, so that can't help. She waves a banner, swings her ponytail, as she dances on Locust Walk beside the sculpture of the broken button. I glance at her, and then only because of the pasties, and I walk on. I'm late for Finance class.

When I come out of class, my friend Dave calls to me.

'Walk me to the library,' he says, looking collegiate as always. 'I need to drop off some books.'

I adore Dave. We've been friends since freshman year when we were neighbours in King's Court Dorm. It's with him that I discovered the joys of people-watching with gay boys. It's ribald, precise, and then over. Exactly my point of view.

As we pass the Palladium, the ritzy on-campus bar and restaurant, my eyes meet those of an Indian girl with hair silking down her back. She's sitting inside by the picture window, staring at me. I look away and keep walking.

'That girl's got her eye on you,' Dave notes, sing-song.

'Not interested,' I sing-song back.

'Not going to dip into your own pond?' he asks, never one to let things go.

I'm amused, despite myself. 'You know I'm racist.'

In fact, I avoid brown people. It's an old habit. I know few South Asians outside my parents' circle of Bangladeshi Muslim friends. Simi and I grew up wary of building friendships within a community that was conservative and often judgmental. When I was younger, a question about studying liberal arts, or being seen in a teen clothing store, might bring on a lecture. Now that I'm drinking and dating, what would my parents and their friends say? I don't have the right lifestyle for a good Bangladeshi Muslim girl, so I live in perpetual fear of having my splintered existence revealed by someone I might mistake for a friend.

I know Simi has a similar paranoia and has kept her life at Hopkins as segregated as mine. It's Maher who appears to manage these challenges more easily, switching between his Bangladeshi and American selves more openly. Even his crew of friends is more brown. Perhaps there is more tolerance for boys living outside their assigned cultural and social paradigms, but I am proud of his wider reach, though I can't seem to do it myself.

Besides, the desis at Penn all seem to know each other already. They dance together in the South Asia Society's cultural shows and escort each other to semi-formal dances. I watch their shows alone in the audience and can't afford fancy-dress parties. And that's the other thing. The Indians and Pakistanis I've met are rich, and I have yet to meet another Bangladeshi at Penn, middle-class or otherwise. And if the desi parents aren't doctors, they are well-to-do professionals, and their children are following in their footsteps – all doctors, lawyers, engineers, and business people in the making.

I'm no different in one regard – I'm in business school. I had thought I would study mathematics, as its elegance and logic had always impressed me. But math alone wasn't enough for my parents to be satisfied with my future solvency, so they suggested actuarial science, a mix of math and business. I ended up at Wharton, and hating my actuarial classes, dropped the major for a concentration in Decision Sciences. It has to do with organizing information, something I'm good at, not that I can yet tell the difference between being good at something and liking it.

As Dave and I near the Button, the Asian dancer's voice floats into our conversation. She's chanting a rhyme about change.

'You can change too,' she says, as Dave and I pass by, her tone becoming intimate, familiar.

I pause, startled. Her face looks tired, but her almond eyes are sharp. She seizes the moment and takes me up.

'What do you think it takes? Do you have to change your name? Your mind? Your station in life?'

I hurry forward, catching up to Dave on the steps of the library, unnerved.

He says, '*She* changed her name.'

'Really?'

'Yeah, her name used to be Kathy Chang. Now it's Kathy Change.'

A limber Chinese boy swoops off his bike as he approaches the racks beside us. Dave's attention shifts instantly.

'Ah, yes,' I note, laughing.

'I know you're a rice queen too. Now, wouldn't he look good kissing me? Or better yet, Glenn?'

I am shocked and delighted, though I can see Glenn in my mind's eye, horrified at the thought, furiously thumbing the curled corkscrew of his penknife. When Glenn was a baby, he had a fleece-and-satin blanket. When the fleece started to pill, he'd pick at the tiny balls and roll them along his tiny fingernails. In grade school, he moved on to rolling the plastic stoppers from the ends of Bic pens along his nails. By college, he had started using the corkscrew of his Swiss Army knife.

I love knowing these things about my first love. It doesn't matter that he's white, a Roman-Catholic-turned-atheist, prep-school educated, suburban American boy, and that I'm brown, a Muslim-turned-agnostic, public-school educated, immigrant girl. That mythical click that my father derides as fantasy, a Western weakness, I have it with him, and no one who sees us together can deny it.

Not that it's been easy between us. On the contrary, we have stubbornly separate politics and our fights are legendary amongst our friends. No one wins a fight with Glenn. No one even wants to get into one. His insults are so pointed, so damaging, yet so clever, they become nicknames and one-liners, no matter how hurtful the initial barb.

It's teaching me to argue better. The black-and-white format I learnt with my parents, not a shred of doubt allowed, it's useless with him. He points out every unmentioned uncertainty, every hole in my logic, every mislabelled feeling, often describing my side before I understand it myself.

Hearing it all so witheringly boiled down would be even more humiliating, if it weren't so illuminating. It's not that Glenn is unemotional. Rather, he's supremely so. His gift is that he can name each feeling, in order of magnitude and relevance, alongside the practical matters.

'Glenn, I don't need you to fix my problems,' I told him when we were thinking about a trip abroad. 'I don't want solutions. I want empathy.'

'But what are you going to do?' The flush of sunburn had evened into a rosy tan across his face. He looked like summer, healthy and hot. 'Your passport's at home. We can't leave the country without it.'

'I'll figure it out, okay? After I'm done being weak.'

'I said you were freaking out, not weak. You're strong. I've always known that. But I want you to be so strong that someday you burn us both up.'

It's unbearable how slowly I learn. Each time I step forward in understanding, I inch back in grace. My fights with my family, and especially with Simi, pain me. I find myself falling back into my old habits, trampling on pros and cons, nuance and feeling, raising righteousness as a weapon. It's only when I see my sister's fallen face that I recall myself, and then it's too late.

By my senior year, everything feels even more polarized. I've stopped speaking to my parents about anything personal, and that space has been swallowed wholly by the question of what I'll do after I graduate college. I am loathe to take up any of the jobs I'm supposedly qualified for, but graduate school looks even more terrifying.

Every afternoon, I go to the 1920 Dining Commons, which is split into two symmetric eating sections. To the right are the blacks. To the left, the whites and everyone else. It's a startling throwback to segregation, self-selected as it is, and has been this way for as long as I've been in school. Several issues of the student newspaper have addressed the divide, but it seems old habits die hard.

I usually sit in the black section because it feels more comfortable than sitting in the white section. But I sit alone, because I know no black students. Until I came to America, most of my friends were black. But my experience in Nigeria is as alien to African-Americans as theirs is to me. And now, I feel like a caricature, clutching at an American accent and Nigerian memories, my meal spiked with Bangladeshi chillies.

I sit down with my tray of food and a copy of *The Daily Pennsylvanian*. There's an article about Kathy Change inside:

she's warning about doing something drastic if things don't change soon. How would, could, should they change, I wonder. What is her Transformation Movement about? I should find out.

When I get back to my room on the 15th floor of the High Rise Dorms, there's a colourful pile outside my door. I nudge it with my foot, and the boom box I gave Glenn for his birthday last year falls to the bottom of the heap, damaged beyond repair. Underneath it is a grey swatch of the boxers I got for him freshman year. Cracked CD cases, ripped up letters, and other burnt, broken, torn, and mangled gifts. In a moment of madness, he has collected everything I've given him over three turbulent years and destroyed them for my viewing.

Glenn was the one who had wanted out. It came as a total shock to me, his proposal that we see other people, but still be friends. I protested day after day, suffering months of grovelling and heartbreak. I'm not sure he understood what he was asking. Neither of us can do without the other. We avoid each other for a few days and then find ourselves back together, talking the same brain talk we've honed and savoured for years.

Finally, I made myself look past him, see other people too. One date with a boy down the hall, and Glenn was back, wanting more, wanting everything. For months, I have heard variations of the same plea on my voicemail, in his wide scripted letters and prolonged emails:

> Olive Witch, we were good together.
> Let's start over.
> I don't know what I was thinking.

I don't know whether I'm ignoring him out of spite, or whether I've fallen out of love. Either way, I can't compete with his loss, much less his destructive grief. I'm too tired to do anything about the pile, so I step over it and go inside.

A brown-and-gold sari drapes along the ceiling of the narrow dorm room, a billowing batik canopy. I strip off my clothes and slide into my unmade bed. At the foot of the bed, there is a six-foot-high window facing west, streaming amber light everywhere. The sheets are warm with the late afternoon sunlight and I am asleep in seconds.

Each bright afternoon feeds a growing habit. The music I play in my room is becoming an addiction. It slows down my work a great deal, and often, instead of studying, I find myself lost in the rhythm and the mourning pop lyrics. But I can't seem to do without it. My superstition is that the music is connected to my heart, and if it stops, so will I. This thought has become so real that my heart jumps if someone abruptly changes or stops playing a song.

The snake charmer's song wakes me from my nap. Tanu's thin fingers resolve in my memory, ivory keys depressing and rising beneath them. The song is playing on a mix tape that Maher gave me for my twenty-first birthday. This version has words and it sounds different in places. But the part with the black keys is exactly how I remember it from the practice room in Nsukka so many years ago. The feeling that comes over me then is such a keen and wordless thing that I am left weak, in tears.

I climb over to the window and push it open. The wind rushes in like a herald. I stand up on the sill and lean out, gripping the inner walls. The ground falls away fifteen stories below. It feels like flying. True to its name, the song winds into itself and around me. The air is icy, but all I feel is the sun on my face and the bass in my body. A small and deadly promise forms in my mind. If the music stops, I will let go. I close my eyes, and in ecstatic terror, I listen.

A faint whirring begins in my ears. It gets louder, almost drowning out the song. The old stories from the Quran come to life. The djinns have come, beings made of fire, who have come to possess us, tell us things we cannot know. And the angels, the wind and the whirring emanating from their wings.

It's deafening now, the music subsumed under the flying sound. I am surrounded by it, by them. On the verge of belief and fear, I open my eyes. The sunlight stabs at me. I see nothing but light. There is nothing but light.

The snake charmer's song filters back into my waking dream. A memory presents itself, muffled but unmistakable. The music had never stopped. Shaking, I climb back down to the bed. The window is another plane, the music the unstable bridge. No less otherworldly is the batik-sari sky of my room. On the other side of my door, Glenn's broken love sits in the shape of mountains. And outside, everywhere, buildings, falling leaves, the real world. Every second counting down.

Next year, I have decided, or perhaps my father has, that I will begin a PhD programme in business at Wharton. The jobs I applied for after graduation were frightening to contemplate doing for long: information systems, technical support, web traffic analysis. I'm praying grad school will be better, or at least more familiar, and of course, it's what my parents want me to do. I have a sinking feeling that either way, I'm out of my depth.

I leave the High Rises and head out to Van Pelt Library with a bag full of books. Inside the library, the dying afternoon turns grey through the dim glass windows. Outside, a giant metal peace sign stands off to the right and people are scattered on the green, lounging on the broken button sculpture.

I notice a frantic knot of people gathering around the peace sign where smoke is wafting upward. I walk over to one of the windows to get a better look. A thin black man is standing under the peace sign, waving his arms, swaying violently. Smoke is pouring off his body. Someone is holding a fire extinguisher, but no one can get close because of the smoke.

I am unable to stop watching, nor do I feel the other students crowding behind me, pushing me against the glass. The man is moaning, or shouting. I can't hear anything he's saying through the window.

Then someone whispers behind me, 'It's Kathy Change.'

The figure of what I thought was a black man morphs into a skeletal dancing body, and my shock turns to tears. What looked like black skin is the ashy and burnt skin of the Asian dancer. The ponytail has long since burnt off and what's left is matted to her skull.

This is what she promised us, her uncomprehending audience – something drastic, something bold, in lieu of, in return for, change. Is she telling the truth with her molten motion? Did she tell it soon enough? Is it an act of engagement, or the opposite?

The paramedics are here now, wrapping her in blankets, strapping her still flailing body to a stretcher. A medic attempts to open her mouth to insert a breathing tube. He grabs her upper jaw and pulls upwards, and her whole face seems to stretch into a howl.

Kathy Change will not survive the trip to the hospital.

the season of floods, 22°C
the crows screech
from the tamarind trees
drunk with the breeze
and the dying light

Dhaka at Dusk

This isn't the summer of my childhood. Simi isn't my constant companion. I can't skip all the afternoon teas and dinner parties and shopping trips to play outside or swim in the pond. My grandfather doesn't come back from his morning walk with hot and spicy dal puris for breakfast. He is not walking with me through my grandmother's garden, tearing off banana leaves and folding them into perfect narrow 'watches' with bands and everything, his bent curly head mirroring my own. Nana has been dead for seven years, but it is only now that I feel it, here in his house, walking through the garden, a crooked banana leaf watch on my wrist. My one context for him is fading from my already faded memory.

But Nanu is here, and she has always been the centre of my Bangladesh experience. Her shuffling walk, her wrinkled hands, the way she croons, *Nanu, Nanu* as she hugs me, harder, longer than I expect. My tiny grandmother is a force, a woman of reckoning. One of the first women in her generation to graduate from college and go on to get a Master's degree, she has spent her life in the pursuit of miracles, not the least of which includes the education of village girls. Nanu traipses from village to village, walks through the grey concrete classrooms with their empty windows and brackish chairs and desks, talks to headmasters, teachers and parents, and finds the girls who might escape child-bridehood. She has spent her life fighting to keep our bony, huge-eyed daughters in school.

I've come to Bangladesh with my mother, just the two of us. It's a treat, a peace offering perhaps, after the horrifyingly articulate break our family experienced the summer I came home from college. Because our finances have been stretched so thin since coming to America, there have been no overseas trips for over a decade for any of us. We used to go to Dhaka en masse as a family, land up there for so long that it became the new normal. Now we are going piecemeal for a month, and it is my first visit as an adult.

I watch wordlessly through the rickshaw curtains at this fiercely alive and pungent place, breathing its last, its first, with every gasping breath. Past the water-stained buildings, the broken-down roads, the paradises of green fields. The rickshawallah's stringy calves pump and pulse under his skin, his eyes bright in his prematurely old face.

'Bangladesh is your home,' my father told me before I left Pittsburgh, in our only exchange of substance since our fight.

I had stood and listened to him only because we had guests. Family friends had come with gifts they wanted my mother to take to Dhaka for their relatives. Abbu went on to tell them, though he was really only telling me, about the letters and telegrams he and the other immigrant East Pakistanis sent to the international media in 1971 during the war of independence, the money they raised, the salaries he and his colleagues gave up for the freedom fighters to help create a brand new country.

'How helpless I felt, so far away, when my compatriots

were fighting for their lives,' he said, his voice orchestral with emotion.

My mother had chimed in, 'We went to Bangladesh, you know, in 1972, after the liberation war ended, before any of our children were born. We had been married just a couple of years and were living in Tripoli at the time. We left Libya and we went back.'

'I wanted to start a ministry for oil and gas mining, to help develop natural resources. But the people in power were not scientists. They weren't interested in my help,' Abbu had said more quietly. 'I felt I was not being of service. So we decided to go back to Africa, but instead of Libya, to Nigeria.'

My mother turned to me, 'You know what the Igbos told us when we moved to Nsukka? Because their civil war, the Biafran war, was still so fresh, like an open wound … When they found out we were from Bangladesh, they said, *you did what we could not.* I never forgot that lament.'

'This is your home,' my father said again. 'You have roots there.' Even though it was no longer clear which country he was talking about.

What my parents didn't tell me was that the years away would leave me stifled by silence, a stranger in my own country. My words halt and stutter, my childhood vocabulary unfit for adult questions. Not that I know what to ask or how. What I really want to know is why I'm so lonely and why the children whisper as I pass.

'They found the boy today,' Amma tells me.

'Who?' I ask.

'The one from the slum who vanished a few days ago. They found him in the pond, arranged with the water lilies.'

I turn to the silent green pond behind us.

'His eyes were empty,' she continues, as if this were a normal thing to say. 'All his soft parts were eaten by the tilapia and the eels.'

The crows flap overhead, black ink against blue sky. This jungle garden, the rippling pond, the wall surrounding, the heaving city. My words, even my thoughts, pale in comparison.

'Do you remember that dance I taught you and Simi in Nigeria? The *Babu Salam* one?' she asks. The memory is immediate, sensate, hazed with red dust. 'I learnt it here, in this house, as a child. After school, I would bike home and my dance teacher would come to the house. Sometimes we rehearsed in the garden.'

There are so few photographs of my parents as children that I have to make them up in my head. My mother is a teenage vision of Simi, with hair like mine except bound into a fat braid. She is astride a bike, sweet and spunky. My father is harder to imagine. Was he ever young? Heedless?

Dhaka at dusk is a mystery, a graveyard, a newborn baby. My grandparents' pond settles into a still mask, and underneath the lily pads, I dream a tumult similar to what's happening inside me, my skin camouflaging livid veins, moulting heart.

I don't know what's betraying me. Somehow, people know I'm not from here. Can they smell it? The sweat that issues too easily into the little hand towel I clutch in my fingers. Can they see it? Some unlikely angle, a betraying hunch or arch in my body, my personality.

There are times when I feel at home. Wearing the shalwar kameez that has become my favourite because of its easy folds, its washed-through thinness. Sitting under the fan whirling at just the right speed to juxtapose the weight of the heat and the snap of cooling wind, teetering between the two like the satisfaction of tears.

And when playing Speed Trump in my father's village home with my cousins, the card game we turn to, driven by language barriers and a need to relate. We call our bets, throw down our trumps, nod knowingly, and in the midst of that, I feel a comfort that's only more real because of its fleetingness. It's gone with the last slap of the cards, and we awkwardly disperse to get ready for dinner.

'Where are you going?' I ask Amma, afraid of being left alone, of being alone.

It's ludicrous because one can't be alone in Bangladesh, not with 140 million people crowded into such a small space.

'To the store down the street,' she says. 'Come with me.'

We walk through waterlogged streets, our rubber sandals sucking, flapping. The corner store is smoky sharp, lit by swinging kerosene lamps. Wheat flour, oil, pickled mangoes, sugar, light bulbs, biscuits.

'We also have to get cigarettes for your uncle,' she says, managing to sound both disapproving and indulgent at the same time.

The man behind the counter adds a pack of Bensons to the pile before we can ask. 'I know what he smokes, Apa,' he tells my mother, smiling. 'Same as me.'

'And I know your mother is as glad about that as I am,' she replies, shaking her head.

Bangladesh is so small, one sprawling family, its secrets abound and ubiquitous. We walk back to the house by the pond, our rubber sandals sticking, slapping.

It's hard to believe that my father grew up in the village, nothing but rice paddies and fruit trees for miles and miles. An older villager squats beside me as I watch little boys play soccer in the sodden fields. He knows my father though he calls him by a name I've not heard before, Kasim.

'We also used to play here as boys,' he tells me, a toothpick waggling his upper lip. His remaining few teeth are stained red with paan, the national betel leaf addiction. 'But we played in the winter, when the paddies were all dried up, not like these hooligans who are ruining the seedlings with their games. Anyway, your father never played with us.'

'Why not?'

He laughs, 'Because he had to study. Kasim was always studying. He said he was going to go to America. We didn't believe him. We didn't even believe in America.'

I can see why. I can scarcely believe in America either from where I'm standing, even though my paternal grandfather was the first university-educated Muslim in the village, welcomed back from his studies with much fanfare and pride. Dada did everything in his power to propel his eldest son into the formidable faceless future. Even more so, I know my father's iron determination first-hand. Yet it's still difficult to see how he left this lush lonely place.

Most of the month that I'm in Bangladesh, I am silent. My mother and I have never known how to talk to each other. For all the conflict between my father and me, we can at least present our cases, however polar, shout out our logic, no matter how dichotomous, and reach our own separate and tragic conclusions. We've communicated, even if there's no trace of nuance, complexity, or emotion. It's all black and white and right and wrong. Feeling, my mother's greatest gift, has always been the first casualty.

When Maher was starting kindergarten in Nigeria, he would

come home every day ravenous, unable to eat anything fast enough. Finally, Amma had asked him if the lunch she packed for him wasn't enough.

'What lunch?' he had replied in astonishment.

Someone, a guard, a helper, a servant, a child, was stealing Maher's lunch before he even realized he had one to eat.

My father was indignant, 'This is outrageous. We must say something.'

'Perhaps I should pack a chili paste sandwich,' Amma said. 'That would teach the thief a lesson!'

We all laughed, but she continued. 'But it must mean someone is very hungry. Maybe it's a child from outside the university, someone who can't afford to bring lunch. I could pack two lunches and tell Maher to hide one, and that way everyone is happy.'

'But that wouldn't solve the problem,' I argued.

In the end, Maher sided with Amma.

'It's mean to make a bad sandwich,' he said. 'I'll just be more careful with my school bag.'

And somehow, the problem resolved itself.

Amma has had allergies all my life, beginning back then in Nigeria and continuing in America. Here in Bangladesh, she's fine, the heat blooming in her cheeks, her movements easy and practiced, her gaze clear. I used to think that her bloodshot eyes were a sign of weakness. Perhaps that's why she asks her questions so plaintively, because she can sense my disregard.

'Listen. I want to tell you something important, and I want you to listen carefully, okay?'

It's as if she doesn't realize that I always listen, that I always have, and I remember every last thing she's ever said. She's so careful with her words and I can't see that it's all consistently about feeling. Instead I focus on the blood lines in her eyes, her thin eyelids, and it reminds me of every time she's loved me, so many times I could die from the counting.

Dusk drapes over the city. Grey, ragged children scream, their hair matted like dry leaves, ghosts darting after each other. A little girl with a palm frond follows, her voice growing faint. They melt into the cooling darkness.

'Listen, okay?' Her voice upturned, but still dignified.

I know it doesn't matter what she's going to say, only how she says it, but I'm oil on her water, too close to the surface to understand, obscuring her reflection with my judgement.

'Something important.'

I want to burst out, say that the only important thing is that we're alive, immigrants being prone to rhetoric or silence, and I'm no different from my mother in this way. But I can't remind her of that, not now, with the red bloodshotness and the almost tears. I imagine something else just underneath, instead of only the dust.

> **Psychiatric Medical Care Unit Patient Behavior Guidelines**
>
> ★ We feel that it is most appropriate to be dressed in street clothes every day – NOT IN HOSPITAL GOWNS.

3.37 p.m.

She's sitting in the lounge with her visitors, wearing mismatched clothes, trying to feel normal. A shapeless candy-striped T-shirt, a long cargo skirt. Her roommate, Young, dropped the clothes off this morning. They didn't let him into the ward, but Wendy gave her the clothes after lunch. He somehow scavenged items from her closet that she hasn't worn in ages, that she didn't even remember she owned. Horizontal stripes? Why did she buy this T-shirt in the first place?

The television blares from the corner, at once comforting and unbearable. The other patients are also by turns unbothered and plagued by its white noise. *Jeopardy!* is on. She used to love the show even though she couldn't answer most of the questions. Now the squares on the board spin and zoom out with such animation, it makes her dizzy.

She will have to purge her belongings when she gets home, although she cannot think about that now. It makes her tired and, in any case, she can't imagine life outside these walls. It's as if everything ends after the hallway where the security guards sit. The elevator doors open and close, but what it looks like on the other side of the elevator is unknown. This place and the real world cannot exist at the same time.

120

The conversation in the room is hushed and stilted, like a bad television show. The people visiting her are like extras, though she has known them for years. Her advisor from grad school, her friends from college, her roommates. It would be more humiliating if their faces didn't look like masks, if their voices weren't muted. Or maybe she's the one with the mask. It papers the entire stretch of her skin.

Visiting hours are almost over. They keep strictly to the two hour limit. She's glad. The smiling is exhausting her.

```
I think I've forgotten how to think
  I think that's how I stay alive
```

rime ice, 25°F
The final scheme is CDMA.
It is completely decentralized and fully dynamic.
However, it has three main disadvantages.
First, few practicing engineers actually understand CDMA.
– Andrew S. Tanenbaum, *Computer Networks*

States of Surrender

At 3 a.m. in Philadelphia, the streets are clear. You can bike down Walnut Street the wrong way from 34th Street to 18th and Rittenhouse Park in less than five minutes. But on Wednesday nights, I don't go home at all. Every Wednesday evening, Sid and I work on our decision processes homework that's due the next morning. Or rather, he helps me with the gist of each problem and I grind through the rest.

Sid thinks in math. Questions about where to eat or whether to meet, which, to me, have no quantitative properties, for him are underlain by probability functions. He finishes his problem set by midnight. At 5 a.m., I'm still not quite done.

I've always been good at gists. I can talk a good talk with the abstracts of a couple of papers under my belt. The thing is, solving problems requires more than a gist's understanding. Late Wednesday night, closer to Thursday morning, I curl up under my desk in my little grey cubicle to escape the relentless office lighting, and I close my burning eyes.

Ever since Mr Eze's sixth grade math class, I've loved math. I saw it as neat groups of numbers that could be rearranged and reduced into one precise answer. I didn't know that wasn't math. Real math, once you get past all the trigonometry and calculus and even linear algebra, is entirely different. First, there are hardly any numbers. And second, there are no precise answers.

In OPIM 900, a doctoral course about decision theory at the Wharton School of Business, our professor is always scribbling stacks of letters and numbers on the board with transfixing speed. They subtract and multiply and differentiate, even on the last line (for god's sake), and all of it balances on a hefty set of conditions.

Such a careful term, *conditions*, never giving away too much, never touching the boundaries, perhaps never even telling the truth. Everything I'm learning in grad school is conditional, in fact, so conditional that what I'm trying to model or predict or influence barely resembles reality anymore.

Who cares if people will choose the blue pill, if they only choose it when they're young and female and reactionary and under the thumbs of first-generation immigrant Bangladeshi Muslim parents? That might tell you something about me, but it isn't going to sell your stash.

I'm also learning that it's not as easy to cram in grad school. When I was in college, I found myself unable to do anything without a deadline looming over my head. The cramming and skimming and last-minute papers worked, barely, no matter that I would have no recollection of them a week later. This isn't cutting it anymore. Just because I've given an answer that sounds halfway reasonable doesn't mean I've understood anything. The professor moves on, satisfied, and I'm undergrad enough to feel elated, but it's like shooting now and bleeding later.

Sid knocks on my cubicle door. 'Are you in there?' he asks. I'm awake in the next second, unable to remember where

I am, but ready to go. I look at my battered Ironman. It's 8.50 a.m. The fuzzy walls of the cubicle focus around me. My homework set needs to be printed out and I have to get to class.

'Yeah,' I call back to Sid. 'Thanks for the wake-up call!'

I hear him unlock the cubicle next to mine and enter. He knows I spend Wednesday nights here but he's too polite to mention it. The printer starts to spit out my assignment as I roll on deodorant. I check to make sure there's paper in the tray and then sprint to the bathroom.

Along the way, I smile hello to another female doctoral student. About five PhD students are admitted to the OPIM department every year, and so far, a woman has been accepted every other year. That makes three of us over five years, plus one tenured female professor in the entire department.

This gender imbalance is old news. The silver lining is that I've never had problems relating to men, not in my adult life anyway. All through college, I hung out with Glenn and his housemates, eight rowdy, sharp, funny men. But Glenn is gone. After our huge fall-out in college, we got back together, and even moved in together after graduation. But now he's joined a field project studying monitor lizards and crows, 9,000 miles away on an island in the Pacific, and he won't return for a year.

Our relationship hiatus is good because I have no time for love. My Phase 1 exams, as they call the oral and comprehensive exams at Wharton, are coming up. I have dozens of books and scores of articles to read in less than a month. It's not nearly enough time to make up for close to two years of cramming.

My reading list for the Phase 1 includes Andrew Tanenbaum's classic 700-page text on computer networks. Each page has five new acronyms, a fact I waste time calculating along with a standard deviation. It slows my reading down to ten minutes a page. Seven hundred pages means 7,000 minutes, or over 100 hours of reading, for one book. I cannot waste a single hour. I sit in my room day after day, night after night, studying and studying and studying.

In winter, Philadelphia is carpeted with black sludge, a mix of snow and salt and dirt. It's not anything like the pretty snowy landscapes pictured in the Western books I read in Nigeria. Here, the trees are shadows of themselves and the sky a dim after-image between the looming buildings. This December is icy and the dropping temperatures reveal more than the painful cold. Branches crystallize and gargoyles screech from the rooftops into the blind white sky.

There is one particularly ghastly monster minding the rain gutters on the building across the street from me. I snarl back at it from my window as I crawl out of bed, light-headed but awake, tired and wired. It's 2.30 in the afternoon and from my window, Rittenhouse Park is a black-and-white photograph.

My housemate, Young, is walking past as I open the door to my bedroom. He starts, 'Jesus, your room.'

I laugh, 'I know it looks crazy, but trust me, it's organized.'

The floor of my room is dotted with stacks of books and articles. It's a map of my research, each outcropping a state to study. I leave him staring and rush to the bathroom. I have just enough time to brush my teeth before jumping on my bike to get to school.

Racing down Walnut Street, the right way this time, my silver bike is a blur streaking through the frozen city. Right before 20th Street, I get stuck behind a bus. I brake in front of an ornate stone-and-brick building which houses the Theosophical Society. I'm becoming obsessed with architectural angles: doors, balconies, window frames, cornices, archways. Research's micro tendency may be affecting my ability to appreciate the bigger picture. But there might be something to these straitjacketed studies. In drilling down to the singular, was there a chance of finding meaning?

I love Philadelphia, even though it gets a bad rap from residents and visitors alike. The weather swings between freezing and burning with precious little spring or fall in between. The crime rate is high and it can't compare with New York's cultural and financial caché. But it's my first home in America, the place I stopped holding my breath, started looking around. Six years of my adult life have been spent here and I have haunts for every season.

'I think you have the potential,' Steve tells me in his crammed office, watching me shift from foot to foot. His twinkly eyes make it look as if he's always smiling through his beard. 'You're bright enough. But you have to figure out what you want. Is this what you really want to do?'

I have two advisors in my department, and both are worried about my progress through the PhD programme. It's not that I'm failing, but my marks are just so, and I'm not doing all the things a doctoral student should do, like reading academic journals and showing an active interest in my field. My half-assed tactics are not helping me 'advance the field of knowledge.' My father's words never cease to haunt me. I had memorized them long before I ever thought about acquiring knowledge, let alone advancing it. His expectations for academic accomplishment have since merged with mine. How could I *not* want to change my world?

'I *do* want to do this,' I protest, tying my hair in a knot at the back of my head, and pulling my neck warmer up around my hair to cool my neck. Last month, I visited an African hair salon on South Street and, after ten hours, two women transformed my waist length curls into hundreds of foot long braids. Braids spill out from the top and sides of my makeshift headband. Its red colour and structured height make me feel like I'm wearing a Nigerian head-dress.

'It's been difficult,' I continue, 'studying for the Phase 1's, and finishing up the directory study analysis for my Masters' thesis ...'

I'm not listening to Steve, or even to myself. I'm spewing a spiel, terrified that he and the rest of my committee will find out that I am incapable, that I'm doing the minimum because that's all I *can* do. For all this talk of potential, of intelligence, they can't know how clueless I am. The longer I'm in the programme, the more precipitous my façade.

After the meeting, I fumble into my cubicle, lean against the door, and close my eyes. How am I supposed to shift my motivation level? Am I in too deep to turn back? I wonder what Nneka, my old friend from Nsukka, is doing, if she's also trying to become a professor, or if she chose medicine or law or one of the professional fields. I know if she were here, our courteous competition would drive me to figure this out. Our friendship, as loyal as it was, was also based on an intense academic drive to succeed.

Two boxy monitors stare at me blank-eyed, beside reams of SAS data and manuals on user interface design and regression analysis.

Get to work. I tell myself, flopping into my chair and switching on my computer. *Stop meta-thinking and start thinking.*

The day of my Phase 1 exams dawns as icy and as fragile as I feel. Stretched and faint from the weeks of worrying, my one consolation is that my colleagues look as nervous as I am. The time slots have been set, and my written exams are first. The first exam is a short-answer test for my minor in decision processes. We are handed little blue books. I silently wish my writing were harder to read, but years of penmanship lessons in Nigeria have left their mark. My errors and fumbles will be recorded in clear stylish script.

The DP test turns out to be surprisingly manageable, posing limited-context problems with multiple tenable solutions. The open form information systems questions for my major prove far more complicated. I waste time making a vague outline, and then pressed by the ticking clock, write down several pages of what I hope will frame a feasible response.

I have an hour to kill before my oral exams begin. To avoid having to talk to the other doctoral students and skyrocket my stress levels, I go outside despite the bitter cold and wander towards the green. My friend Dave has been working at Van Pelt Library since we graduated, and I go inside to find him.

'Hello, Nubian princess,' he says from behind the reference desk, all preppy and peppy.

'What?' I say confused.

'Quick on the draw today,' he winks, and points to my braids.

'God, don't tease me about being clever. I'm about to commit academic suicide. My oral exams are in an hour.'

'What are you doing here then? Shouldn't you be sacrificing your first born to the devil? Oh wait, you already did that when you joined Wharton.'

'Tell me something new.' I'm hoping Dave's brand of careless risqué humour will distract me from my sense of impending doom. Sure enough, he obliges.

'Remember that MTV VJ you think is hot, Simon Rex? Well, I found out he used to be in porn.'

'You're kidding!'

'No, and you're in luck. I found out which video he's in. We can rent it the next time you come over.'

I leave the library feeling slightly lighter. Ivy-clad buildings surround. West of the library is the peace sign, metallic and stark against the ice. Wreaths of flowers ring its base where Kathy Change set herself on fire. I look at my watch. The minutes have ticked by far too quickly. I trudge back to Wharton.

When it comes time, I enter Vance Hall. Four professors sit in a huge, empty lecture room with their notepads and glasses and messy hair. They include both my advisors, my decision sciences professor, and an information systems professor. The scene is theatrical and, for me, traumatic. I'm not good at performing, on stage or otherwise. The only time I do it is when I sing with the University Choral Society. But then, I'm in the midst of a hundred people, the altos alone numbering over twenty, my voice a sliver in the tree of song. I've never gone solo. Not like this.

The first question, about online consumer behaviour, fells me. It's obvious to everyone that I am nervous beyond belief. My mouth is parched, and everything I have learnt seems locked in an unreachable part of my brain.

Data mining, electronic security, organizational processes, operations research.

I nosedive from there. The words swirl in the air, detached from any meaning I can glean. It's even worse when I'm the one speaking, like I'm creating my own monsters, ones whose names I know but can't define.

Business flow modelling, interface design, consumer behaviour, usability testing.

'Why don't you try answering that question from the perspective of the supplier?' My other advisor, Jerry, is trying to help, referencing some past discussion he and I have had. I remember snippets of possibly relevant conversations, but in my panic, I don't know which one to use.

Statistics, online purchase tracking, experimental economics, emerging markets.

'How is marketing research relevant to this topic?' the decision sciences professor grumbles.

I know his query is a rebuttal of my last response, not a friendly pointer. I digress, floundering further, struck by the sensation that I am speaking in tongues, when I can speak at all.

New media strategies, decision theory, e-commerce, information search costs.

I don't know how the time passes, but somehow, second by humiliating second, it does. The professors try their best to keep the session relaxed and brief, but when I am allowed to exit the room, I am certain my doctoral studies are over.

I'm wrong. To my great relief and more than passing horror, I pass my Phase 1 exams, albeit conditionally. Over the next year-and-half, my workload becomes even more unendurable, like fighting through a briar forest to its impenetrable centre. More than ever, I am less sure of what I'm doing, and it's making me reckless and dissociated.

On weekends, my centre city apartment is often packed with dancing revellers and little cliques. Young is pumping the keg for our ultimate frisbee friends. College friends who have graduated and work in the city are drinking cocktails in the hallway. My PhD colleagues are crowded around a couch talking about our upcoming Phase 2 exams. The stereo is blasting dance music and the TV is playing the *Matrix* on mute.

Dyan arrives high on heroin and weed. He heads straight to the booze table. He's a new friend and I am still getting used to his drug use. Not the drugs, but that *he* does them. I had always assumed kids who grew up in Bangladesh would be more conservative than the Bangladeshi kids growing up in the States, but I'm sorely mistaken.

Dyan has brought a friend with him. Shra is also from Bangladesh. She's wearing a gold threaded sari blouse that stops just below her breasts, and skintight jeans. Her lips are painted a slippery red and her hair spills from a loose knot at the back of her head. She's studying fine arts, and she tells me in her lazy stoner voice about her spring break trip back home to Dhaka. On the flight over there, she got wasted.

'I hate flying sober,' she says winking.

I nod even though I've never ordered alcohol on a plane.

'But can you believe the nerve of this Biman stewardess? She baulked at serving me!'

I have no answer to this, because drinking anywhere near Bangladeshis would not even occur to me.

'Although they'll jump to serve the men,' she continues. 'Typical.'

Here I spent my teenage years, hoping my parents wouldn't catch me swearing or wearing a short skirt or hanging out with boys or thinking about studying languages. There Shra stands, a drunk art student, her midriff unrepentantly bare, smoke curling out of her pursed mouth. All those parental threats of sending us to Bangladesh when we misbehaved – maybe we should have taken them up.

Dyan pulls me into my bedroom, 'Hey, I heard one of your roommates has Percocet pills?'

'I could ask,' I say. 'But aren't you fucked up already?'

'Like you aren't either. I can see you watching your hands move.'

He flops down on my bed, below a ficus tree strung with Christmas lights. Under the pillow, he discovers a small leather covered box. The box is shaped like a teardrop and the leather decorated with an intricate pattern, a typical Bangladeshi design. My grandmother gave it to me when I last went to Dhaka. He shakes the box and it rattles. I take it from him and open it. The lid comes off silently, revealing a carmine velvet lining. Little blue pills roll around, dull gems against the lining.

'Vikes?' he asks hopefully.

'Sleeping pills,' I answer.

Every night I take the leather box to the fire escape. I light matches, let them burn down to the edges, and I wait for sunrise. City sunrises are unspectacular, the usual fireworks obscured by a scrim of smog and skyscrapers. I wait, despite the overwhelming grey, because it marks the end of the darkness. Each dawn, I allow myself to unpeel one blue capsule from its shiny foil cocoon. I put it into the crimson body of the teardrop box. It's my pleasure, my reward for watching another night die without me.

'If you smell the inside of the box, it smells like peace,' I tell Dyan. I hold the box up to his face.

He sniffs and then says, 'Sugar coating, woman. That's what you're smelling.'

I grin. Dyan's gift is that he judges nobody. 'There's a painting upstairs on the tenth floor which you'd like. Come see?'

But Dyan is mesmerized by the lights on the tree, unable or unwilling to move.

I grab a pink cotton blanket from the bed and leave the

party unnoticed. The stairs are cold under my bare feet and I run up them to get to the carpeted hallway of the tenth floor. Our upstairs neighbours have strange and arresting art. Paintings and sculptures line the hallway outside their apartments. My favourite is the blue painting. Tonight, when I see it fishbowling across the wall, I feel as if I've never really looked at it before. As I crouch in front of it, the blanket puddling around me, I see a night sky with stars streaking across its body, dark and radiant. The silver points drift deeper into the turbulent sky and the painting becomes a living thing.

I start to feel a little dizzy and tear myself away. Out on the fire escape, I automatically look for the box of matches, my burnt match castles. But I'm not on my floor, and the black metal landing is clear. I keep climbing the fire escape until I get to the roof. I push the door, and it opens with a screech. Centre City fills my vision.

For the millionth time, I wish I could channel Glenn. But after seven years, we've decided to call it quits, at least romantically. Glenn is gone again, on another set of field trips, one project studying owls in the Oregon woods and another on wolves in Ontario. His chosen field of wildlife ecology fits him, his body always in motion, his love for the outdoors. We joke that his old freshman year moniker, Wolfman, has actually become his fate. But his profession doesn't make for stable relationships, or even regular conversation, so we come to a mutual amicable parting. It takes our friends by surprise, their grief eclipsing ours.

'We're still friends! Why so sad?' I protest, even though the loss is yet unmeasured inside me.

'You don't know what you had,' Alexa says almost in tears. 'It was so beautiful.'

'It was also bloody! You were all there for the fat girl fight. That one lasted years.'

Glenn, whose beautiful athlete's body has never let him down, is ever disparaging of everyone else's physical flaws, his judging a constant bone of contention between us.

'It was more perfect than either of you guess.'

They're right, but it's not Glenn's presence I crave, because in a way, he's always with me. What I need is Glenn's unrelenting rationality. I'd use that ruthless self-awareness to change my life. But I'm having trouble identifying my options or my feelings, which was Glenn's shining talent, the ability to explain himself in the plainest words, expressing feelings most people would be too unaware or embarrassed to say out loud.

I'm disgusted because you used
the dish sponge to wipe the floor.

> *You're guilty because you should have*
> *come home when you said you would.*

I'm afraid because time is so very long,
and I don't know how much longer I can
live with all these dead spaces in my heart.

I want to stop everything, because despite agonizing thought, I don't know what else to do. Music, engineering, French, business, athletics, teaching, English. Nothing seems right, but I cannot quit without a plan. Even with one, it's going to be hard to face my parents. Simi had her next step all mapped out, and still, furor.

'Drawing!' she bursts out over the phone when she calls me. 'That's how Abbu described my career of choice: *drawing.*'

Simi has just dropped out of an engineering PhD programme at Carnegie Mellon so she can become an architect. I can hear my father's voice, accented and accusing.

'Well, Abbu always did know how to bullet point.'

'It would be nice to get some support.'

'Yeah, well good luck with that,' I say amused, knowing she'll hear the sympathy in my voice. 'Anyway, he should have known from the beginning you were going to be an architect. Remember when you used to steal his blue print paper and draw houses on it? You were like five. If that isn't a calling, then I don't know what is.'

'What?' she says astounded. 'I did that?'

'Yes. And your drawings were pretty good too.'

'Why didn't you tell me this before? I could have saved myself six years of cut-throat engineering education, two degrees, and two more years of shitty work experience.'

'Sorry, baby sister. I thought you needed to learn things the hard way, like every other middle child.'

'Thanks a lot,' she says, hanging up, laughing.

If I can't even tell my sister, what could I possibly say to my parents that would make up for yet another child quitting a PhD programme? To boot, I'm almost four years in. My last conversation with them was like every other one before it.

'I'm not sure if this is the right programme for me, Abbu.'

'How is your research going? Is your advisor helping you?'

'It's fine. Both my advisors are great. I just don't know if I can do this.'

'Of course, you can. You can do anything you set your mind to. Can't you, my first-born, my daughter?'

The force of all my parents have done, every luxury and advantage I have been gifted, pushes me to speak.

'I can.'

I need to think more clearly, with more courage. Or I need to stop thinking, finish this doctorate, and then take a break and figure out Plan B. The opening prayer of the Quran comes to me, the one that asks for direction, a guide to the straight path, the one of favour, not of wrath, nor of those who go astray.

I remember the notebooks Simi and I had when we were children, in which we copied down surahs, supervised by my mother. We penciled the Arabic transliteration on the right, the English translation on the left, and memorized both. My favourite surah was Surah Al-Lahab, The Flame, which started with the word 'Perish!' and dealt a series of terrible curses on an evil man and his wife. The last line, 'a twisted rope of palm leaf fibre round her own neck', was one I found frightening and fascinating.

When we left Nigeria, we continued our Islamic education at a local mosque in the suburbs of Pittsburgh. Every Sunday, my siblings and I would grumblingly rise, get driven forty-five minutes each way for three hours of Quranic and Arabic classes. It wasn't just the time that we protested. It was also that many of our classmates were equally unhappy with their required attendance, and eager to show anyone up. Simi and I were older than most of the other students, so we were generally left alone. But Maher, traumatized by his snotty peers, developed a hatred for Islamic instruction that followed him into adulthood. Ironically, he has also grown up into the only one of us who prays.

I can pinpoint when I started losing my religion. The first crack came when I learnt about Islam's inheritance and witness laws which treated a woman as worth half a man.

'But why?' I had asked my father, all teenage stridence.

'Before Islam, women weren't even allowed to own any property. Even in the West. It was a revolutionary shift.'

This explanation satisfied me for a few more years, and then only because my parents had never showed any signs of treating either me or Simi as worth half Maher. In our family at least, nothing less or different was expected of daughters. Indeed, Maher with his less-than-stellar grades was often compared unflatteringly with his older sisters.

Then, in college, my fights with Abbu about Glenn started. His effort to force his own religious model on me led to a slow cataclysmic burn. It would take me years to internalize my feelings of betrayal, longer to reject the religion that turned my own parents against me.

Other than when I visit my parents, I haven't been to a mosque in years. I've broken every rule there is, drinking, dating, dissembling about it all. Surah Al-Kafirun, the prayer of the unbelievers, is the only surah I can still recite without guilt. As a child, I used to like it because it repeated a line, which meant one less line to memorize. Now the prayer has become a shield against those who would spurn me, either on religious, social, or intellectual grounds. The last line reads, *La kum deenu kum wa liya deen: To you be your way, and to me mine.*

In Rittenhouse Park below, a stone lion arches under a molten yellow spotlight. The darkness is colouring in the winter, the skyline etching itself against a purple-haze sky. Towards the west, a new skyscraper has launched beside the river, every window lit up. The time, in giant neon numbers, spins around its apex, like a weather vane, except it's pointing to the hurrying future. I pull the blanket over my head and a deep pink sky floods over me. Light pierces through the weave, like stars.

When I drag myself to school the next day, the afternoon is dripping, dying. The sky wilts above my head. It's easy to step back and watch myself going through the motions. Friday, I was a dancer, an escapist. Monday, I'm a graduate student with all my props: three-ring binder, small grey cubicle, and piles of data logs to analyse. Lunch in the doctoral lounge, office hours in the computer labs, and in five odd years, a diploma in my pocket.

Tuesday, after classes, I'm an athlete, practicing twenty hours a week with the Philadelphia women's ultimate frisbee club team. It's the sport that's taken the place of swimming. Glenn taught me how to throw during freshman year, and ever since then, I've been addicted. I carry a frisbee everywhere I go.

But it's gotten much harder now that I'm playing with the nationally-ranked city team instead of the smaller college league. I'm no longer the go-to girl with the hands of glue and the half field huck to the end zone. The Philly women I play with can run faster, jump higher, lay out farther than I can dream. They're insane athletes with attitudes to match. My spot on the team is continually in question. Unlike my swimming coach in high school, the Peppers will cut anyone at any time if she isn't pulling her weight, rookie or not.

I don't sleep for more than a few hours at a time. I skip breakfast, inhale lunch, and after school and frisbee practice, I'm so tired that I sometimes fall asleep before dinner, still wearing my cleats. I jerk awake at the witching hour, tense and disoriented, wash my face, and start my never-ending reading list.

Today is Wednesday, and I'm a scientist, mixing whatever we have in the liquor cabinet with whatever we have in the fridge. Young has made a pitcher of iced tea, condensing on the top shelf. I could have iced tea with a splash of rum. Or club soda fizzed into Peach Schnapps. Or maybe two drops from the tiny bottle Dyan gave me, 'for special occasions', chased with a shot of vodka.

It's not that I'm looking for escape. I'll leave that for the weekends. Tonight, I'm restless, and there's no one to say no.

I make dead sure that no one knows my secret, that I'm cracking up. I can't let it get out. The despair, the anger that overcomes me every time I stop to notice – it's not original. It can't be real, this grief that everyone's already felt, written, filmed, sung a million times over. Nothing is mine alone, and even then, how could I despair when my life is yet so charmed? I am housed, fed, funded, educated, loved. Everything spirals up. It makes my growing depression feel ridiculous, my words useless, making much of ordinary emotion.

My other fear, cavalier and conceited, is that I've already done what matters, or whatever matters when you're twenty-five. I've accomplished all the goals I was set so far, and I can see the rest of them standing in a row, falling domino by domino. I can feel myself fading. I am so tired, and nothing stops the march except sleep. All I want is to close my eyes for a second, for a year.

In one of my classes, a graduate psychology course, we're doing memory experiments that prove that we see much more than we remember and we remember more than we can say. For 250 milliseconds, the world is stamped onto our retinal palette, in all its minutiae. Then in less than the space of a blink, a sweeping destructive descent of an eyelid, it's gone.

This is what I want. A world that recreates itself, every time my eyes open to the light. Not one that magnifies from the past, nor one that telescopes into the future. I want something untouched by anything except the immediate now.

I take my chaser and go outside. The streets are long soft mats of asphalt, tassled by trees. The city screams through wrought grillwork, wooden shutters, gabled turrets. I stand transfixed by a statue of Pegasus. His bronze blood is draining out of his body, dripping off the tips of his hooves and wings. The setting sun catches the dripping blood on fire. I know the Pegasus isn't even painted, so it can't be a trick of the light on peeling paint. I try to unsee it, but the blood keeps draining and dripping. I reach my hand out. Old gold light and blood melts onto my fingernails.

I remember the little zoo in Nsukka, and the first place I'd run to, where the python slept. It was like a wide well, shoulder high, with a crosshatched wire roof. I'd gingerly stretch my head over the metal grill to look down into the snake's house. The sight never failed to thrill and terrify me. A monstrous python, coiled round and round, its tail disappearing into the bowels of the well. Its head was as large as mine, and if I picked an unlucky vantage point, a poison breath away. I never once thought about how it must be for something so large to lie in a space so small that it had to spiral itself forever.

I cannot visit zoos anymore. I know the good ones do damage control, research, and rescue from extinction. But all I can think of are bony mangy lions, the crowded monkey house, the hyenas ceaselessly pacing and laughing, and the python cornered in its concrete cage. Even sculptures of animals will make me remember, a stone lion, a bronze Pegasus. That frozen motion, a captured life.

I am thirteen again, trapped in a system, unable to break free. Each solution I envision comes with a set of conditions that render it untenable. I stay in school and I stifle. I leave school and I'm lost. I stay open to possibility and I'm incapacitated. I leave myself closed and I perish. There are no equations that resolve to a result I can bear. I can no longer rely on religion, nor even on the heart. And now that the science of numbers and reason are failing me, I am losing faith in the rest of it.

conditional instability, 98°F

she's a fast acting fuse
she knows what to do
in this century
of high loss and gadgets
she spins the dial
on the potentiometer
and if the needle
on the high gain signal amp flies
she switches off the surge protector
her isolation transformed
but sometimes
even with the precision lubricators
she'll arrive at a standoff
uninsulated
that's when she pulls the plug
flips on the resistors
a female quick disconnect

Limbo

I'm putting on eyeliner. Clinique in new black. My eyes are burning, circled. I figure I'll make them look purposeful with makeup, but my hands are trembling from the drugs. I went into a mental hospital with a black eye and came out with a sheaf of prescriptions. Anti-depressants, anxiety medication, sleeping pills. The worst part of a failed suicide attempt is how embarrassing it is to be alive. I stand in my room with the curtains drawn, eggshells all around me. I can't look anyone in the eye.

It's already been six months since I left the hospital. It's only been six months since I left the hospital. Sometimes I imagine I'm still in the psych ward, playing cards, waiting for lights out. Sometimes I don't believe I was ever there. How does someone do something so extreme and go on to live a normal life? Is this a normal life? Can anyone tell that I'm mad? That I'm still not sorry, but not so sad?

'Hey, are you in there?' Young's booming voice pierces my bedroom door.

'Come in,' I say, dropping the eye pencil on the dresser, watching its reflection tumble and multiply in the opposing mirrors.

He looks in, 'Dude, it's dark in here. What're you doing? Are you coming?'

'Yeah, I'm coming, I'm coming.'

I thread my cleats through my backpack strap and pick up a prescription bottle. There is an open space on the rug where I was sitting, but otherwise there is stuff everywhere. Books, papers, and clothes cover the hard wood floor, the bed, the top of the dresser. Unlike before, there is no mapping, no method to my madness. It's strictly a mess.

Young watches as I pop the bottle open and swallow a pill, 'What is that?'

It's the third anti-depressant I've tried this year. 'A new anti-depressant,' I say. 'I didn't like the last one.'

'What was wrong with it?'

'Sexual dysfunction was one of the possible side effects. I didn't want to deal with that. I have enough problems.'

'Good one,' he says amused.

I like Young tremendously. He's easy going and puts his stupendous memory of pop culture trivia to hilarious use. As a housemate, he could be a little cleaner, but I'll take his funny, matter-of-fact manner any day.

Outside the day lets loose. I hunch down into the passenger seat of Young's Honda Civic. The wind is too free with my hair, the sky too open. The Pet Shop Boys is playing on Young's car stereo. And by playing, I mean blasting. I think we've all memorized the words to 'Go West' from the sheer repetition. I've heard that Koreans love bands like the Pet Shop Boys and Erasure. It's like their gangster get-down music.

I look over at him. Young is tall for a Korean and he looks as if he's folded into the car seat. His hair sticks straight up and his skin is like honey, darkened by the sun. He has his usual outrageous gear on, lime-yellow basketball shorts, an orange tank top, and a visor turned up.

He knows what I'm thinking and says with gusto, 'What? This song is great, isn't it?'

I smile and shake my head, looking back at the road. It was Young who found me passed out after swallowing all my blue killjoys. He visited me in the psychiatric ward every day after that. His brisk light way of speaking almost makes it easier to talk about feeling and not feeling. Almost.

I think things might be worse in these months after leaving the hospital than they were before. I have a small private kingdom of friends who know what happened. They call, visit, watch over me, forming a web so close it's hard to imagine that I arrived at this place without anyone the wiser. But I've been practising disguises for more years than not. I can put on any face with its matching mood and modulation. It's become so that I can't tell if I exist anymore, if who they're watching is even real.

My parents are mute, silenced by my sudden and violent

expression of grief. When they drove from Pittsburgh to visit me in the psychiatric ward in Philadelphia, they looked older and frailer, while Simi and Maher looked absurdly young. The hour we spent together was harrowing. We sat in a windowless conference room, unable to say anything to each other.

In the last few years, I've fallen out of touch with my family. Part of it has been tactical, to keep my secret American life safe. Part of it was revenge, on my parents, for their rigid understanding of the one right path, for their rejection of me and mine. No small part of it was being young and stupid. I've even drawn away from my sister, who has always been resolute in her support of whatever I do or desire. And Maher was so young when Simi and I left for college that in a way, he's had to grow up an only child, at least in his teenage years. I don't know who he's become.

Now when we talk, it's all parables and pleasantries.

'How are you?'

'I'm fine. How are you?'

'The world keeps turning.'

And I don't know how.

Glenn's anger ignites from thousands of miles away, as bewildered and alienating as my family's speechlessness. We've been in touch as much as his fieldwork allows, but as per long distance friendships, it's not easy to engage on the day to day.

'What the hell? What the fucking hell? You couldn't have told me, written me, something? Before *this*?' he bites off the word.

I know where he's coming from. Like many of my close friends, maybe more than most, he feels betrayed by my silence, by my fall. Our no-holds-barred relationship lets him say it in his shotgun caustic way. Besides, Glenn has never understood withdrawal as a strategy, let alone depression as an illness. His empathic powers only go so far.

'I tried to tell you I was having trouble. You told me to get over it.' I can't stop the sharpness in my voice, even though I don't blame him in the least. I know this is a bed of my own making.

And I'm simplifying what he said, rejecting all the solutions he offered for my half-articulated malaises. I'm disappointed he couldn't just let me feel, and angry at myself for I don't know what. Failing. At living or dying.

He simmers to a low boil, hearing every spoken and unspoken inflection in my voice. 'You know you're everything, right? You don't need me or anyone else. You can do this or anything else. But you can't die. Don't you fucking dare.' His voice cracks.

I say nothing.

'Can you hear me?'

I can't.

The therapist I'm required to see every week tells me that even if suicide is premeditated, the actual act is often an impulse, a whim. It was true for me. I thought about it so much that when I finally did take all those pills, I wasn't sure if it were another dream, that I wouldn't stop just before doing it. And the frantic swallowing once I started – was that a double dare in my head or something with more integrity? And there's the real problem, that I think wanting to die might have integrity.

When Young and I get to the fields in Fairmount Park, I sit in the car while he gets our gear from the boot. As he walks away, he turns to look at me. I nod and he nods back, walking on. The fields are filling up for summer league, frisbees flying overhead. I take a breath as I climb out of the car, feeling as if

I'm gathering myself together, ill-fitting pieces. Outside, the wind is flirty, changeling. A tricky day for disc.

'So where've you been?' a teammate asks. 'What's the story?'

My story to everyone not in my throne room is that I fell and knocked myself unconscious and woke up coming out of a cat scan, and I don't remember how I fell. It's all true, but I'm leaving out the bit about swallowing a few dozen sleeping pills.

The player offers the usual reaction, 'Christ! How are you now?'

'Fine,' I say, shrugging.

I don't mind telling this veiled story. The truth is so close around my words, yet barricaded away. The contradiction makes my skin crawl. That and the black eye I sported for weeks looked cool.

'Fall in!' the captain shouts as the drills begin.

I used to hate running because it was so hard, so heaving. It took me years to get into good enough shape so that the thought alone wouldn't terrorize me. Now, in small bursts, I enjoy it. Motion has nothing to do with thinking. That's the beauty of it. How did I forget those hard won lessons from swimming in high school? That swift slice through water, that endorphin rush.

The next time you think you can out-think your problems, I tell myself as I slow down from a sprint, *you should go running or swimming instead*.

When I started college, I was far away enough from my Nigerian childhood to leave it unspoken. Bangladesh came up only because of my skin colour and was easily dismissed because I had never lived there. It was my parents who were from there.

I assembled my American accent, my assured American attitude, and conjured who I thought was the perfect person:

someone who was bold and whimsical and passionate. I climbed into her skin and wore it until it was mine. After a year, I didn't have to think twice about what was coming out of my mouth. After four years, I stopped being surprised that people believed this person was me. All that seems like a memory. When I speak, it seems like an echo of my former self, a washed-out version of a made-up character.

Wharton has granted my request for a leave of absence, ostensibly to get some rest and perspective. I know I'm not going back, even though I'm almost four years in and my Masters' thesis just got published. No one, least of all my parents, might understand why I'm quitting now, but at least no one will question me anymore. I am being left to my own means, and my decisions, right or wrong, are finally wholly my own.

Whatever my means, they are not being aided by sleeplessness. I finally have time to sleep, my consummate pleasure, and I cannot. I've never had insomnia before. I never thought I would because I was chronically sleep-deprived. People with insomnia used to strike me as curious artistic types, finicky in some fundamental way. Now I'm one of those people.

Most nights, it's too hot in my bedroom, even when the air conditioner is on full blast. I close my eyes and awaken an hour later, the night wide and portentous, licking its lips. I slip out of bed, grab my Discman, and wander down the hallway to where the computers hum in their heated crowded space. As I sink into the yellow velvet couch, the green glow from the monitors flickers through my eyelids. The musicians cry into my ears.

I don't understand my pain. I tap my calf, punch my thigh, hit myself, in rhythm, and then in tears. I want the bruising on the outside to suck out the one inside. Sometimes I feel as if I haven't stopped crying in years. Other times, I feel so dry and empty, it's worse than crying.

'How often do you feel down?' my therapist asks me once.

'I don't know,' I say.

'Once a day? Every few days?'

I think about the reverse. When did I last feel joy? I can't remember. I know it can't be true, but it feels like I haven't been happy in years.

Young's room is cold. He has a much smaller room than mine and his mattress is on the floor, college-style, so the air conditioner works well. I close the door behind me and crouch down beside his bed. As my eyes adjust to the darkness, I see him asleep on the bed, gold skin and spiked black hair. I touch his arm. His skin is silky smooth.

'What's wrong?' he asks, making me jump. His breath is as cool, cooler than the air.

'I can't sleep,' I whisper.

'Even with the sleeping pills the shrink prescribed?'

'I took two tonight, and I've been awake for hours.'

'Okay, okay, don't take any more.' The irony of being prescribed sleeping pills after having overdosed on them is not lost on either of us.

Years of sharing beds in motel rooms at tournaments, of sleeping against each other in packed rental cars, have made physical closeness among my frisbee crew a natural thing. Young pulls me across his body, and I let myself drift and sink. The air-conditioned air rolls over us, and I let it go, the heat outside, the burning of my eyes, the wideness of the night.

When I tell people I'm going to chop off my braids rather than have them taken out, they look at me as if I'm crazy. It had taken an entire day to plait my hair into scores of foot-long braids, months ago, and I know it will take less time to unbraid it all, but I can't stand the thought of sitting for so long. Instead, I stand for half an hour on old Philadelphia Inquirers while Saira brandishes scissors around my head.

If it hadn't been for the ultimate frisbee team at Penn, Saira and I might never have met. Even if we'd been in the same graduation class, we would have moved in different circles. Saira is a trust fund baby, goes to exotic locales on holiday, and is an English major. But these things we have in common – we have both secretly dated white boys, we love dancing, and we're both daughters of South Asian Muslim parents. Saira's Pakistani-born parents are even stricter than mine. She and I understand each other implicitly, recounting our parallel histories only for comic relief.

With each metallic snip, a braid falls to the floor.

Saira is laughing. 'It looks crazy!' she exclaims. 'I don't know if I like it, but it definitely looks cool.'

It feels strange to be able to run my fingers through my hair after having braids for so long, even stranger to run out of hair after an inch. I haven't had short hair since high school, almost a decade ago, and it was never this short.

But there's another reason I've cut my hair off. My entire adult life, I have been defined and described by my hair, braided or loose, dyed or black. It has become more powerful than me and I want to get rid of it to prove to myself that I don't need it. As futile a move as when Glenn burned and broke all my gifts to prove he didn't need me. I'm yet too raw to see past skin.

I step off the newspapers and look at the damage. The braids lie there, limp and lifeless. I feel vindicated in getting rid of them, but before I trash it all, I pull out the longest, neatest braid. I'm a collector, but this is my first lock of hair.

I'm going to keep it to remember my power by, if indeed, somehow I have cut it off.

When I show up to my first day of work at a new startup, my boss Ana takes one look at my new hair and breathes a sigh of relief.

'Thank god!' she exclaims. 'The angel investors are here to check out the new office. My first employee with dreadlocks wouldn't make the best impression, even if you do have two business degrees.'

'They weren't dreads, Ana. They were braids.' But she doesn't hear me.

Tugging at my hair, I walk over to the corner of the large room we've hired for the offices of Chaitime. As per the flat hierarchy of the day, all the desks are in the same room and there are no dividers. Programmers, graphic designers, content producers, marketers, business development – everyone next to everyone else.

I like the social and managerial implications of this layout, but it's also disconcerting because I'm still having trouble with open spaces, as if I'm on the edge of a precipice and could stumble at any moment. Even my bedroom seems too big sometimes, so I've fortified my bed with pillows and a stuffed frog half my height that Glenn sent me. I make a warm little cave for myself every night before I sleep.

At the Chaitime office, I hang a large tapestry behind my chair like a curtain. It's not as private as four walls and a door, but it's better than nothing.

I met Ana, a volatile visionary Indian American and the CEO of Chaitime, through her husband who went to Penn with me. We ran into each other on the street one day and she offered me a job almost too good to be true: content manager of a website portal with a six-figure salary. It's a position that involves writing (something I've always enjoyed) and business (my last eight years of education). And it gives me something to do until I'm ready to think again. So far, I've been subsisting on tutoring rich Wharton kids for rent and food money, which fits my transient state of mind, but I know I have to move on.

Chaitime's target audience is one of the wealthiest minorities in the country: South Asian Americans. From the beginning, I have trouble replacing the term *Indian* with *South Asian*. I have spent my life lumping myself into ill-fitting categories. In Nigeria, I was Bangladeshi, even though I had never lived there. In high school in America, I was from Nigeria, because that was where I had just come from, the only place I had lived, the country of my birth. When I got my US citizenship midway through college, I became American. I stopped mentioning Nigeria because it was too complicated to explain why I was from there but looked otherwise. Easier to invoke my Bangladeshi heritage, though not trivial.

Bang-la-what?

Bangladesh.

What language do they speak there?

Bangla. Bengali. Same as Calcutta in India.

So it's part of India?

At Chaitime, everyone knows where Bangladesh is. It's one of the seven countries listed in our company mission statement: Bangladesh, Bhutan, India, Nepal, Pakistan, the Maldives, and Sri Lanka. Geographically, it sits waterlogged, almost landlocked, in the eastern armpit of India.

The company's first big marketing ploy is based on my sister's road trip around the country. Simi is about to move west and join UC Berkeley's PhD programme in architecture, but before she does, she's planned a two-month, 7000-mile journey around America in her little red sports coupe. Neither of her decisions sits well with our parents – drawing for a living, much less the concept of a joyride. Amma is also worried about her baby daughter driving all over the wild west on her own.

Ana's match-making brain wakes up when she hears Simi is both single and not averse to meeting new people. *Seema's Quest* is an online column with Simi going on dates in different cities with desi boys and writing up the experiences. Her columns are brutal and hysterical, and a taped conversation with one of her hapless dates in a New York City restaurant is downloaded hundreds of times. I'm not sure why people sign up to be part of the *Quest*, as the dates are so public, even if we do change their names. But they do, and our promotion is off to a running start.

My first fight with Ana accompanies the death of the *Quest*. Simi has tired of it and she wants to go on a national park jaunt through the Northwest without thinking about how to trash her next suitor.

'She can't quit now!' Ana exclaims. 'We've already set up the next two suitors. Tell her she has to finish at least these two.' Ana doesn't like her plans changed. She is even more offended when it's by someone else's direction.

'Ana, she doesn't want to do it anymore, and besides she's off radar now, somewhere in Oregon. We can come up with something else to replace the quest. Shreyas is on the website's Youth team and is great with video and webcams. We're thinking – *Real World* like on MTV but for Indians, I mean, South Asians –'

'Are you even listening to me? This is unacceptable! We've negotiated ads in *India Today* for the *Quest*. You have to be able to carry through with projects. Not dump them when –'

Ana hits a nerve, and my voice rises accordingly, 'Carrying through with projects is what I'm good at, Ana!'

As I say this, I'm acutely conscious that I quit my PhD four years in, on the tail end of my seven-year romance with Glenn. I am in between lives, nowhere I planned, and totally unnerved. But it remains that when it's not that important to me, like working for a startup, my paralysis of options, my fear of mediocrity dissolves. It's easy then to have the kind of flippancy and flair that web development requires. At Chaitime, I'm hyper-efficient. I'm a fixer bar none.

My fights with Ana follow a predictable pattern: we disagree in some fashion. She throws a tantrum and fires me. Or I quit, saying I'm going to go west, like Young's favourite song. I'm only half-joking. Then she calls me up and apologizes, and I reluctantly leave my hermit cave bedroom and return to work. We compromise or we don't, depending on who is feeling generous, and we start over, no lesson learnt.

I'm feeling better slowly, and sleeping longer, but it's surprising how little it takes to make me jittery. One of my pacts after leaving the psych ward was to stop pretending. If it's a moody day, it's a moody day. I tell my friends, one by one, face to face, so that it's a promise not just to them, but to me. *I will not lie about how I am feeling.* Some days, it takes tremendous effort to keep my face still, other days even more to show expression.

In any case, *Seema's Quest* is over. After all, without her cooperation, it's useless, and since we aren't compensating our dating queen for her efforts, she drives away without guilt.

On the momentum of our South Asian 'Real World' marketing extravaganza, Chaitime expands into India and the UK. It's the eve of the 21st century during the internet boom, and venture capital money is flowing like water. I get to visit and train staff in Mumbai and London, and we set up marketing offices in Los Angeles, New York, and Toronto.

Picking our RealWorld interns is an eye-opening experience. Of course, our participants are successful students. They're South Asian Americans in university in the States. There is almost no other immigrant group more ambitious. But what Chaitime is looking for is verve, originality, and shameless self-promotion. I add my own bias to the selection process. It's been almost a decade since I started college, but I'm hoping to find something different than what I was surrounded by, than who I was myself, then. I scour the applications for artists, actors, activists. It isn't easy, and right off the bat, I have to give up on finding any Bangladeshis. Hundreds of applications in, I find a student who isn't studying a liberal arts subject as an aside to his or her professional goals.

'A straight up music major, Shreyas! I can't believe it. I've never heard of a desi music major.'

I'm watching a videotape of a skinny South Indian boy wearing huge headphones and grooving as he raps.

'I don't know why you're so surprised. You know the arts are a huge part of Indian culture and history.'

Shreyas was born and brought up in Chennai. He's studying physics, but I hired him for his impeccable writing and his video skills.

'No, it's not that,' I say. 'All the Indians, I mean, South Asians – they're all studying to be high-powered professionals.'

It's true. It's why Chaitime has even come into existence. There is a lot of South Asian American money out there.

'But you know that the Bengalis are renowned for literature? For their poetry? Your countrymen,' Shreyas says.

I didn't know this.

For the first time, I wonder what it would be like to live in Bangladesh, whether it would make any more or less sense than living in Nigeria. After avoiding brown people for so long, afraid of their judgments and circumscribed perspectives, I'm surrounded by them, and it's a relief. I don't have to explain why I heap chillis on take-out food, what a water pitcher is doing beside the toilet, how I can love and hate America, hate and love Bangladesh.

Even more unexpectedly, Chaitime affords me the return of my Nigerian identity. I no longer have to leave it out just because it's easier not to explain.

'Where are you from?' I ask our saucy new marketing researcher who has a Gujarati Indian name.

'Kenya, darling,' she says with her charming East African accent, easy modern poise.

'Is that where your family lives?'

'The whole rotten lot.' She swings her shampoo-commercial hair off her shoulder.

'Have you been to India?'

'Never. And where are you from, pretty?'

And for the first time in years, I speak the motley truth, my accent effortlessly sharpening back into the slow Nigerian cadence of my growing up years. When I think about Nsukka now, it is with an unreasoning nostalgia. I know none of my childhood friends live there anymore, that our old house must be occupied by other tenants, the classrooms full of children a generation below me. But it remains my favourite daydream, walking up Ako Okweli Street towards the tennis and badminton courts, the music building where I used to play the piano, the back fields of the primary school where we played oga and other clapping games, and the jungle beside our house where we ran wild under the setting sun. I promise myself that one of these days, I will gather the courage and money it would require to return.

The tech boom has a familial bonus: I get to reconnect with Maher. He's in college, at the University of Pittsburgh, and as addicted to the Internet as I am. Online chatting has gotten us past the hurdle of only speaking during my infrequent trips home, Pittsburgh itself a limiting factor. Memories of my miserable high school years and continuing tensions with my parents make me unpleasant company. I regress into my old teenage ways, sullen, quick to anger, seemingly unable to help any of it. It's almost as if I get to throw off a heavy hooded cape each time I leave Pittsburgh. I get to become myself, or someone else, whoever I want to be. The informal and written format of online chatting makes our reconnection even easier.

'Following footsteps, are we?' I type into our chat screen.

Maher is at the University of Pittburgh's business school, and has chosen information systems as his major.

'Oh, yes, you've been an excellent role model,' he fires back. 'I've learnt so much.'

'I'm waiting for the drop.'

'Well, given yours and Simi's successive failures to complete grad school …'

'Ouch.'

'I have enough ammunition with the 'rents to argue against going to grad school myself. Thank god, because I envision a long life of prosperous corporate peondom.'

I score Maher a summer job at Chaitime and he comes to live with me in Philly for two hot humid months. It's perfect because the Real World interns are also around, and he's always been good at engaging, especially with second-generation immigrant kids. Technically, he's one himself, even though he spent his first six years in Nigeria. But Maher is Brooklyn born, his accent resolutely Pittsburghese.

I don't know if it's living in Pittsburgh, on the borders of middle America, or growing up between our parents' immigrant ideals and my minor rebellions, but my little brother is a centrist, in the most generous sense of that word. He can do something I can't. He can live with both sides, and even more amazingly, he engages with a light-heartedness I have yet to learn.

The Internet bust comes so soon after the boom that my two years at Chaitime feels like playing in the school grounds, making up games. Rumours fly thick and fast about layoffs, and then it starts happening. I am resigned. I have no idea if I'll make this round or the next, and frankly, I don't care. I've done the Wharton job, so to speak, and earned enough money to pay off all of my student loans. I am debt-free. When I'm called into the glass-walled conference room, I'm only mildly embarrassed, and more than a little relieved.

To celebrate and commiserate, I throw a Chaitanic party. I've recently moved into my own place, a lovely seventeenth storey apartment on Arch Street with stunning views of Centre City. It's become a gathering spot over the last year-and-half, and everyone knows where everything is. A marketer enters and heads directly to my kitchen to start mixing drinks. The news team is downloading the latest Bollywood songs, and our favourite film, *Office Space*, is playing on the TV.

Shreyas is standing in the long hallway connecting the living room with my bedroom, reading the reams of butcher paper taped to the wall, from floor to ceiling.

to say my hunger is so old
crystalline precise
I know what I want
two of you, one of her
my hand in my pocket

When I first constructed my word wall, I had considered putting it in my bedroom rather than in the hallway. Most of what I'm writing is despairing, love-struck, lost. I figured most people wouldn't be interested in reading it. I was wrong. People seem drawn to despair, love, and loss, and everyone who comes to my flat reads my wall. I've even hung a tin box of markers nearby for people to add to the jumble of words and colours.

'Do you want to write something?' I ask Shreyas, offering him the box of markers.

'Do you feel exposed?' he turns to me, all unqualified attention. 'Your thoughts out there for everyone to read?'

I admire Shreyas' writing, his filmmaker's eye. But it's his dense voice, his skin so heated to the touch, that gets me now.

'It's not a journal ...' I say, 'More like pieces of poems. To kick-start me into writing again. I used to write a long time ago.'

'What did you write?'

I wince. 'Poems, all rhyming, all precious. I think I'd die if I had to read them now.'

I thought I'd be safe
  from the American drawl
    from the click shut locks of the clique shut halls

'Why did you stop?'

'Because every time I sat down to write, I felt like it had

to be good, and I had to finish it. But this wall, it's all rough paper, so what I write can be rough too …'

she sits on the bed
as the rain counts out
the minutes of her life
on the tin roof
dhip dhap

I'm winding a curl around my finger as I talk. My hair is longer and dyed a fiery red-gold. Shreyas pulls at my hand and our arms fall, linked by little finger.

My word wall is working. I'm writing again, after so many years. I'm not sure that any of the hundreds of snatches of poems will ever grow to a single complete thought, but the riot of words and colours makes me feel accomplished, in a way that nothing in the last decade has done. Even the very act of writing makes me feel better.

He turns back to the wall, 'You should do something with this.'

'I should be a writer …' I say offhand.

It's true
I'm not lost
I know where I stand
I'm only waiting
for lightning to strike

Shreyas looks at me, 'I think that's clear to everyone except you.'

It's only then that I think about writing as a career instead of a hobby. And in my mind, time that had felt so out of control, life so long and labouring, it unwinds and stretches, the hours filling wholly, easily, joyfully.

> *Look again.*
> *The lightning is only waiting*
> *for you.*

I select an orange marker and I sit down by the wall.

iridescence, 72°F
patchwork coats matching
hibiscus with satin
tarweed boutonnière
the fog bank draws near
the evening is here and spreading

Dahlia High

The dahlias are in bloom. From afar, I can see a large vibrant splotch of colour, next to the greenhouse in Golden Gate Park. As I walk towards the garden, the patch resolves into individual paintings, each flower riotously distinct in shape, size, and colour. A miniature coral reef, made of petal and leaf. Here, powder puffs in magenta. There, a spiky sunny explosion. And now, I'm close, too close to breathe for the beauty.

It's my second year in San Francisco. I've come here to write. Because I don't know what to write about, I've joined an MFA programme, at the University of San Francisco, so someone else can tell me what to do and when to do it.

'Hell, it's so stunning, I can't take it.'

I hear Resbalador's familiar surfer-boy voice from across the dahlia garden.

'Don't cry just yet,' I say laughing. 'You haven't even seen this side. There's a lady bloom here who will break your heart.'

Resbalador is in my writing programme, and it was his idea to visit the garden. He's wheeling his chair to the other side, as captivated as I am. His long dark hair gleams in the sunlight and his head, dahlia high, vanishes around the corner.

There are so many things that have disappointed me over the years. My family's insistence on the one straight path. My inability to force my mind to function well in business school, leading to my heart giving in. I'd always thought my body at least would play along, that motion could be my last stand.

It was only after meeting Resbalador that I realized what it meant to return from my death wish with a body as coordinated, internally and externally, as before. Resbalador sits in a wheelchair, paralysed from waist down from a daredevil river diving accident when he was seventeen. Because I didn't know him then, I cannot translate his utter vitality, twenty years later, back into his teenage years. His life force is so potent that to match it with motion is an audacious leap. He makes me understand that not even movement is a holy grail. For him, it's art. His music and his writing are urgent, piercing, more engaged than I had thought possible. Listening to him, it's not hard to conceive of a life's work concerned with finding beauty.

There's a fence around the flowers. I lean down over it and the taller blooms brush against my face. Would anyone notice if I ate one? If I opened my mouth and bit the velvet bitter petals? As my lips part, I hear a sound. It's so far away that I mistake it for a memory. Then it clarifies into something present, unfamiliar. Not the primal lockstep beat of village drums, but something more prideful, joyous, something young.

I tear myself from the garden and start towards the beat. On the path, beside a giant green trash bin, is an orange dahlia with a broken stem. Inside the bin are more discarded flowers, clippings cast off by a choosy park gardener. I pick up the orange bloom, holding her under her flounced petal skirt, above the break in her stem, and I keep following the sound.

This is the first time in my adult life that I'm alone. For the last ten years, I have grown up, into, and out of lovers. But here, on the western edge of America, I am no longer anyone else's dream. My last love, Shreyas, is still finishing school in Philadelphia and even though our break was difficult for me, I know it's for the best, especially since he's moving back to India soon after.

It feels good to start over, and for the first time since adolescence, I'm getting enough sleep. It's one of the rules I made for myself after leaving the psych ward. No more alarm clocks. I wake when I'm done sleeping, no matter the consequence. It means I go to bed earlier, or I work part-time, or I get to class late, or I miss dates. It doesn't matter, as long as I get as much sleep as I need.

What luxury, people exclaim, when they hear of my sleeping religion.

'No,' I protest. I say it over and over again, to remind everyone, most of all myself. 'It's not a luxury, sleeping enough. It saves my life. And it might improve yours if you try it.'

I'm exaggerating, but only a little. Fatigue doesn't catalyse my depression, but it spirals it to hell right quick. Getting enough sleep won't prevent my fall. It'll only slow it down. It's just one of the pieces of my madding puzzle and it hasn't stopped me from hoarding my killjoys. I still have one box of sleeping pills hidden under my mattress. I'm not yet strong enough to stop counting ways to die.

Sleeping is helping, but sleeping alone is another story. I hadn't realized how warm my lovers had kept me. Every night, I shiver myself to sleep, cupping my nose against the drafty windows. Northern California isn't warm and its homes are even less so. Temperature control marks the lone point of contention Simi and I have. After a decade apart, we're living together again. We're overjoyed at being reunited and it feels like the very air is pressing back in pleasure. It's just the thermostat that gets in the way.

'It's warm enough,' she protests when I go to turn up the heat.

'You're wearing three layers! Indoors! That's why you think it's warm enough,' I shoot back.

'And you're wearing only underwear. We're not living in the tropics anymore. You could calibrate a little.'

'How is it that in ten years in Philly, I was never cold indoors, and now in California, I'm freezing my ass off?'

'Buildings are overheated or overcooled on the East coast,' she says, in her architecture professor voice. 'Americans are wasteful with their energy consumption.'

'I'm getting a portable heater for my room,' I say. 'Plus an electric blanket. Put that in your energy budget.'

'I will consider all of this,' she says seriously, 'when I design your house.'

Simi is doing a PhD in architecture at U.C. Berkeley while simultaneously getting a Masters in architecture, a separate professional degree. With a Masters in engineering already in hand, she is single-handedly advancing the field of knowledge for all three of us. Maher and I are more than happy with this state of affairs. Less pressure on us.

Of course, our cohabitation is not like before, two twin beds in one room, the jungle whispering outside. On the best coast, as Simi calls it, we have our own flat with our own rooms, our aesthetics designated by décor. Her bedroom has bare white walls, a jar of sharpened pencils on a shelf, a neatly made bed, and a closet arranged according to the colour and length of her clothes. My bedroom is dominated by a batik print canopy. My bed is never made, and strewn with clothes, pillows, books, and handwritten poems and notes.

Now that I own a camera, hundreds of photographs tile my walls. Some are of friends at parties, but here and there are streetscapes in motion, the silhouettes of objects, the myriad turns of sunset, the photographs that are becoming part of my remembering arts.

Our parents aren't thrilled that we've both moved so far away, to the other side of America. And California's multiple fault lines are no solace to my geologist father. The silver lining is that Simi and I are together on dangerous ground, so we can look after each other.

Maher, with his usual backhanded approval of anything I do, voices only taunts about West Coast bleeding heart ideals. When it comes down to it, all three of us, and even our parents, would make most of the same moral and political decisions, but we talk so differently from each other, it's hard to see this.

It's 4 p.m. And the sun's heat is dying. A chill wind flirts in and away. San Francisco's witching hour is not at midnight but mid-afternoon, when the fog starts rolling in from the sea. Golden Gate Park is on the front lines. The far edge of the park starts at the Pacific Ocean and reaches back inland some forty blocks, ending in the Haight. Like a giant green scoop, it ladles equal parts sunshine sky and sea foam fog on its own body. I go everywhere armed with layers of clothes, a sweater for the morning, a T-shirt for the afternoon, a jacket for the night.

The pedestrian walkway pulls me and my broken dahlia through soft stretches of grass, between flowerbeds of vermillion and flax. Who am I to say that it's me and not the earth that's breathing, that the dahlia didn't pick me up on its way to the music?

By the time I reach the drummers, I've pulled my jacket from my backpack and zipped it up to my chin. The hat Simi crocheted for me is drawn down over my ears. Only my hands are exposed because I'm holding the dahlia.

There are more than two dozen drummers on Hippie Hill today, all with drums of different sizes but more than requisite energy. A cymbalist is lying flat on his back propped up by the hill's incline. His eyes are closed, his cymbals by his side. I sway to the swelling beat, the familiar feeling of connecting with sound stealing over me. I learnt how to dance in my bedroom in high school. Over the years, it's proved easier than athletics, more ecstatic than drugs, longer lived than orgasm. It's given me a body deep understanding. Given street music, fleet light, I could dance till dawn, stone cold sober, diamonds in my eyes.

A low growling begins, flooding around my ankles, rising up. It's coming from a didgeridoo player, who is holding his enormous wooden instrument, his arms loosely vined with tattoos, tight with effort. I know him. Scott is a funny, lanky writer in my programme. Here, he is all bass. I can almost see the hollow spaces in his body widen and tighten. He starts so deep, I don't notice until I'm already trembling along the blown notes.

The crash of the cymbals is like a cloudburst, a shock. The cymbalist is standing, his glittering metal discs clapped together. The sunlight is strong again and the dancers are coming, two by one, three by two, from somewhere inside the woods into the clearing. They aren't in my climate. I'm in the middle of a West Coast winter but they're standing at the edge of summer. Their limbs are scratched and bare, sun burnished, clothed in that ragged chic of the Haight, their hair tangled and loose. Who are they? Do they live in the woods? Were they waiting for this moment, this call to motion? It doesn't matter. I dance with them corybantic, heated and damp inside my jacket. I hold my dahlia up to the clouding sky.

I knew the instant I got to San Francisco that this place was closer to home than any other I'd had in America, even though it was like nothing I'd ever seen. The city is arresting, unwinding. My first afternoon, after unpacking my boxes, I stepped outside into a stillness and light unlike anything I had experienced in fifteen years on the East Coast. A crumpled Beetle rumbled past me, careering around a corner plot choked with wild thorny roses. Up high the blue blue sky. Below, the cold brown ground.

The people I meet have wide wale: writers who come to class after surfing, programmer photographers, doctors with drug addictions, single mothers who investigate more than their teenagers.

'You're leaving already?' I say to a fellow dancer at the Makeout Room. We're in the Mission, where everyone goes for late night tacos, to visit thrift stores and bookshops and cafés, for dancing and the best margaritas. It's my favourite part of the city, sunny, bikeable, and the grungiest, hippest, least gentrified of its neighbourhoods. Simi and I want to live here, once she's done with her coursework at Berkeley.

'Yeah, I'm going on a hike up Mount Tam tomorrow, early,' she says, draining the last of her drink.

In the last two years, I've heard every organic excuse under the sun. Yoga, community service, gardening, sailing, mural painting, skiing, cooking, wine tasting, the list goes on and on. It's so earnest as to make me gag. It's so earnest as to persuade me.

When I move to the city, my fourth year in the Bay Area, I do it without Simi because she's moved to Oakland with her new boyfriend, a sharp beautiful man, also doing a PhD at Berkeley. My parents approve of him, despite the fact that he's a white, half-Jewish American.

'Are you kidding me?' Glenn exclaims when I tell him this news. He's engaged to be married and lives in Canada now. We rarely see each other, but when we talk on the phone, infrequently as it is, the hours slip by, vibrant and joyful. 'Your parents, who couldn't even say my name out loud, they *like* him?'

'Well, he *is* doing a PhD in Chemistry, and my parents are education snobs.'

'It's not just that,' he says flatly. And he's right. No amount of education would have made Glenn a suitable match back when we were together. Our family was too close to FOB then, my parents swinging between fear and loathing of their adopted country's cultural mores.

He continues, 'You tell your sister and her boyfriend that they are walking on my back, on my blood and bones. Yours too.'

His melodrama makes us both laugh, but it's a sobering thought, not the least of which of what could have been.

After graduating from writing school, I land a job managing the front office of a science company. The work is part-time, secretarial, and I love it. Organizing is one of my fortes, and I find it infinitely satisfying to take a mess and marshal it into method. So far, I've been successful in finding part-time positions with benefits and which aren't corporate. This ensures me just enough money to cover my bills, though sometimes not even that. Either way, I have that diamond of a prize, time. Time to write, take photographs, sleep eight hours a night.

My new digs in the Mission are lux. I have my own marble bathroom, shining red-wood floors, a granite kitchen, and there's an elevator in the building so Resbalador can come over. It's a pity he's not there the night I catch my hair on fire because, in his prescient way, he would have understood immediately what it meant.

'Parfois j'aimerais mourir tellement j'ai voulu croire …'

I'm dancing around my bedroom after midnight, my usual pastime after a night out, singing Manu Chao in pitiable French. Even if I don't count the years of learning French in Nigeria, I went on to study it to fluency in high school in America, along with Spanish. In the years following, my linguistic memories tragically degraded: French and Spanish, the Bangla my parents used to speak to me, Arabic script from Islamic school, my childhood apprehension of Igbo, and basic Japanese from a high school summer programme. At age eighteen, before entering university, I knew seven languages in one form or another. Now I'm down to one.

'Je ne t'aime plus, mon amour … Come dance with me,' I entreat my old friend Campbell who is sprawled on the bed. Campbell is Korean American, a charming brilliant nihilist who I've persuaded to my ecstatic dancing ways. He went to Penn with me, one of my few friends from Wharton and that only because we were in the same dorm freshman year. He also moved west around the same time I did and has recently quit his management consulting job to become a professional poker player. This choice gets him askance looks from others, but to me, he seems happier, and as well off. Maybe more so.

Campbell shakes his head, 'I can't move.'

Candlelight throws our shadows at the walls, covered with butcher paper, the word wall I keep constructing, flat to flat, city to city, ever since the jumpstart one back in Philly. When the music starts to fade, I leap over to my stereo to hit repeat. I know it probably drives my flatmate and neighbours crazy, but I'm one of those obsessives who plays a tune over and over again, days, weeks, sometimes months on end.

In my haste to restart the song, I don't notice my hair oscillating into the candle flame, smoking and crackling alight. Campbell does, or at least smells it before I do.

'You're on fire!' he shouts jumping up.

I find his outburst hilarious and collapse into a useless giggling mass as he claps out the flames on my head. I am unhurt, but the burnt rubber odour is terrible, and singed clumps of hair fall off in the fray. Luckily, I have enough curls to make up for the loss, and I even manage to pass out despite the smell.

The next morning, I drag myself out of bed, wash my hair, and get to work hungover and still smelling of smoke. Things have been more difficult at my job the last few weeks, as I've been assigned marketing tasks in addition to my usual office management work. It's not the actual marketing work that's hard, nor the additional time required. It's the concept of marketing that gets me. It reminds me of persuading people to purchase, of profiteering. It was at Wharton that I learnt the awesome and alarming sophistication of marketing. How colours could create desire. What precisely placed images might allay fear. Which carefully worded questions would change your very mind.

Of course, it was also Wharton that taught me that even writing is a business. Everything I learnt about supply and demand, positioning and preference, markets and consumers, it all applies. I play the numbers game when I send out literary submissions, I know not to take rejection personally, I record each gain and loss in a spreadsheet, I move on.

When I get to work, my boss comes to my desk with a huge stack of folders. The smell of burnt hair amplifies in my aching head.

'Agenda item #1 for today,' he says. 'New business development.'

Dread starts to fill me. When I was working at Chaitime, time and again I refused promotions to business development or executive management, because I liked my content management job just fine. It seems I might not have the choice now.

He continues, 'We need more clients. We can't afford to hire anyone else, and you have the background to do this work.'

He's right, and I make a split second decision. 'I'm sorry,' I tell him, genuinely so. 'I can't do this. But don't worry, I'll find someone who can to replace me.'

When I get home, my flatmate has news. Instead of renewing our lease next month, he wants to move in with friends in Noe Valley.

'My life is falling apart,' I tell Simi on the phone. 'I have no job, nowhere to live, no partner.'

'Don't be silly,' she tells me. 'Who just got her first print publication? Who finished writing school in the prettiest city in America? Who lives large and lovely?'

She's right, but it doesn't stop me from despairing as I dismantle my room. I sell or give away almost everything I own, except for books, photo albums, and journals, which I mail to my parents. Amongst the books, I tuck in a lock of braided hair, every letter I've ever received, mix tapes from Maher, a tattered frisbee jersey, and one orange dahlia pressed between the pages of a journal. Of the ten boxes I mail to

Pittsburgh, most contain keepsakes I can't bear to throw away.

On the last day of the month, I stand on a blue-collared cliff and say goodbye to the best coast. On the other side of America lies my recent past – intense, intellectual, intolerable. Here, between the sea and the mountain, I can be both dark and quiet. I am nothing and for as long as I want.

bow echo, 73°F

> I hate thinking. I hate decisions. I hate planning.
> I hate organizing. I hate persuading. I hate responsibility.
> I hate doing all these things my father taught me to do.
> Most of all, I hate feeling, my mother's offering.
> I hate all the things I am and could be.
> And these are all the rational reasons for my grief.

6.23 p.m.

They've given her a blue folder to put her writings in. Her new favourite colour. She puts the Paxil pamphlet in it. Outside her window, the buildings are unfamiliar. One has gargoyles on its edges. She knows this city well, but she cannot tell where she is. She decides to memorize the façade but gets bored counting the gargoyles. She picks up a magazine. She can't remember the last time she read for fun. It's her attention span. She can't concentrate for long.

Psychiatric Medical Care Unit

TO OBTAIN AND KEEP PHONE PRIVILEGES

* Spend time out of room interacting with peers and staff.

Wandering out into the hallway, she sees Mary and Jim playing gin rummy in the community room. They've tried to make the room inviting, but it still looks formal and smells clinical. Square corporate chairs, bars on the windows. Jim invites her to join the card game. She's forgotten how to play but it comes back. They keep up a steady patter that's unintelligible but comforting. The cards smack down lightly on the coffee table. A Mona Lisa queen, a throne of diamonds, a seven of

spades. A Jack swoops down and off the table, settling on the
floor unnoticed. She thinks about flying. Or is it falling? Or
dying. It's been whole minutes now since she thought of dying.

> My hair smells like the ocean. My legs are restless. My brain
> feels slow. My hands are shaking. My eyes are tired. My voice is
> hoarse. I keep getting lost in my head. Where did my gods go?
> Where did I?

Jim leans too close to her, and watches her too carefully. She
imagines he's a prophet.

'You're in no-man's land now,' he says. 'Nothing you say will
be overlooked. You don't have to pretend anymore.'

She says nothing.

He continues in his disjointed way, 'You're special, see?'

She looks at him.

'Because you got close to God.'

What does he know, she wonders.

> Is it physical or is it mental?
> Am I really mad? Why would I leave
> this place? I'm afraid of regret.
> I'm afraid I won't do it right.
> I'll be back and have to do it again.
> I can't tell if I'm looking
> for signs to die or signs to live.
> The fact that I can't tell
> the difference is disturbing me.

> I think I might be
> fucking stupid

This is a Window

never getting lost
never getting found

—*Uche Nduka*

haze, 30°C
the crows swoop and cry
dust whips off their wings
in slow motion
the water stained buildings remember
the rains

Enter the Living World

I am hurrying through the damp sweating halls of Zia International Airport. I can feel the heat already. My flight was three hours late, but a barrage of cousins and aunts and uncles have been waiting since morning. The baggage claim area of this airport is little more than a warehouse. An ancient conveyor belt winds through the centre of the room carrying a curiosity shop's worth of luggage and ware. You'd never guess this was the beginning of the 21st century. My black Samsonite, ordinarily indistinguishable, sits starkly prim in the array. The other bags and boxes are worn and bulging, bound with multi-coloured ropes. A row of clear plastic jugs carrying some unknown liquid slides by.

When I turn around, the exit catches my breath. The outer wall is made of glass, fogged with the humid air outside and every viewable inch is crowded with people. There seem to be a thousand eager faces looking in. Somehow, my relatives emerge from the mosh of waving limbs and craning heads as I walk through the doorways. I am embarrassed that almost none of their smiling faces are familiar to me, but they know exactly who I am. Speaking all at once, they take my hands and bags and sweep me from the terminal into the outside.

It's an even bigger shock to enter the living world that is Dhaka. The air is palpable, the sky a blinding blue. Beggars, young and old, catch onto the edges of the dupatta wrapped around my head, tugging at my free hand. I know that from now on, I won't have an unobserved moment.

Being the centre of gawking attention is only the first of my worries. I have never been connected with Bangladesh. In my family, I am the Nigerian child, born in Igbo-land. I had even called myself an Igbo name, Ngozi, as soon as I knew what names were. This is one of the reasons I can't quite relate to my father when he talks about roots. His nation is vivid in his voice, despite decades spent living elsewhere. My nationality, my accent, changes with the landscape, with the very weather.

Six of us pile into a dilapidated car. I sit awkwardly on my suitcase, getting a whiff of the potent air. The pollution here is powerful and the trailing edge of winter exacerbates it. Without the rain to tamp them down, shrouds of dirt rise two stories in the air and scatter, an almost beautiful hazed vision. My throat starts to itch.

We career through the streets at great speed. Wide as the roads are out by the airport, they are jammed with overflowing buses, cycle rickshaws, three-wheeled baby taxis, trucks full of anything from bricks to livestock, and other cars like ours: overstuffed, wheezy, oil-dribbling contraptions weaving in and out of the traffic.

I have my camera out, nose against the window, but it is clear that a point-and-shoot is not nearly enough to capture even a fraction of what I'm seeing. I need a full-scale movie crew, aerial cranes, and digital video. What I don't need is Photoshop. The colours are brighter than real.

The walls of every building are marked with water stains, and through the dust, the lush of the countryside is startling. Even in the dry season, it's obvious that this is a land of floods.

We pull into a small neighbourhood in Uttara, inside Dhaka's northern city limits, and into a gated compound. In the spilling chaos of baggage and bodies, I find Raan, my two-year-old niece, at my side. She's watching me, chubby and solemn and curious. Dark eyes, darker skin. I am instantly enamoured. The gleaming complexions of my Nigerian classmates are standards of beauty set too long ago to change. Even as I sweep her into my arms, her critical elders are complaining.

'She's so black! You should use Fair and Lovely on her.'

'Don't let her run around in the sun!'

Bangladeshis elevate fair skin. The words for beauty and fairness are used interchangeably. As the older, darker, more serious sibling in the family, my role, growing up, was fixed long ago, as were those of my siblings. I was the smart one. Simi was the pretty one. Maher was the loved and loving baby. Because of the way families brand you, my siblings and I are forever doomed to struggle to display all the other dimensions we might have. Couldn't I be pretty? Couldn't Simi be smart? Couldn't Maher make good on his own? Oh no.

In Nigeria, black skin was tantamount to affirming identity, but lighter skin was rare and revered. The opposite but equally strange phenomenon prevailed in my high school in Pittsburgh. My classmates would spend hours roasting in the spring and summer sunlight to 'get some colour'. All these countries obsessed with skin colour different from the norm and the natural.

My cousin, Raan's mother, smiles at me, unmoved by the commentary about her daughter. She married late by Bangladeshi standards, her own dark skin marking her for less, despite a lovely rounded face, delicate pixie-like features and a gentle generous demeanour. I was angry then about her plight and am furious now about the comments about Raan. But how can I start a fight so soon after my arrival, when I don't even know my place? I hug Raan closer and move into the shade.

The next morning, I wake to the beginning of a siege. The house is clattering with activity. Everyone is home because of a hartaal, a country-wide strike called by the opposition party in protest of the policies of the ruling party's government. No one is supposed to be on the roads from sunrise to sunset and all businesses and schools have shut down for fear of assault or vandalism.

Sunlight splays on my bed, sliced into paisley shapes by the grills barring the windows. Outside, a lone rickshawallah is plying his trade, ferrying a brave or foolhardy passenger. My lively teenage cousin, Shamayla, bounces into my room, having waited hours for me to wake. She was chauffeured to Uttara last night from the neighbourhood of Gulshan where the wealthy and the foreign ensconce themselves.

'It's Valentine's Day!' she exclaims. 'But the hartaal means we can't go to school to exchange our valentines.'

I laugh. How and when did Valentine's Day make it here?

'At least the teachers will be happy,' she continues. 'They hate Valentine's Day. They hate anything western.'

I don't tell Shamayla I hate Valentine's Day too, with its chocolate-covered Hallmark packaging. But the holiday is just beginning in Bangladesh, and besides, nothing could or should dissuade a teenager from her romances.

'Maybe this means Valentine's Day will go on for the entire month,' I tell her. 'Or at least until the hartaals are over.'

Sure enough, the hartaals do go on, day after day. We sit at home and wait for the evenings, when we can go outside. At night, Dhaka's numberless corner stores stand out, lone light bulbs casting shadows everywhere. I could stare at the crammed shelves for hours: Nido tins of powdered milk, Ribena blackcurrant juice, fist-sized batteries, sturdy matchboxes. Anachronistic and faded, the odd years of my childhood are on display.

Shamayla confirms a bit of youthful Bangladeshi life that I had discovered through Dyan and his candy-red lipstick friend at Penn: rampant intoxication among the elite.

'There's an orgy tonight at this guy's house,' she says, too casually to mean the word she's saying.

'What happens at these orgies?' I ask, unable to imagine much sex going on.

'Doping and binging.'

'Which means?'

'People drink, smoke, kiss, you know.'

'Smoke as in cigarettes, or pot?'

'Both. But mostly cigs. *Everyone* smokes.'

'You too?'

'Not like three packs a day like some people. Just a few when I'm drinking. Some people do heroin too. Wanna go?' she asks eagerly.

'I'd love to, but I promised I'd go to this other party with your parents,' I say with real regret. I'm dying to see the scene.

That evening, I accompany Shamayla's parents to a private party of a high-ranking government official. I've grown close to Shamayla's mother, my accomplished and gorgeous Tilo

Aunty. She's my mother's cousin, but in the way these things go, her family is as close to me as my own. Plus she delights in western culture as easily as she lives in the east, so I don't have to explain or edit myself as I do with most others.

It's funny how this time in Bangladesh differs from the last. More than a decade ago, I came to Dhaka with my mother for the summer, pining and possessed in the way only heartsick twenty-nothing-year-olds can be. This time I've come alone, for a year, maybe more, not for a treat or to escape, but to write and take photographs. I've even dreamed up a project, a collection of short stories interleaved with photographs. But I don't care what others expect. It's my own private experiment, no prize or punishment at the end, or perhaps a little bit of both. This lack of tether is a different kind of heartsick.

My aunt and uncle's Pajero zips through the city, guided by their able driver. After 9 p.m., the roads are clear, though during the day, they are almost impassable. A journey of a few kilometres could take hours at 4 p.m. As we pass through Tejgaon on our way to Dhanmondi, there's a long line of parked rickshaws hinting at a slum nearby. Rickshawallahs are the most numerous of Dhaka's manual labourers. Their straining bodies fill the streets, night or day, each fare worth a fraction of a meal. The street lamps throw lush sodium light on their decorated hooded cycles. At night, they are chained facing each other in pairs, lovers in lockstep.

By the time we arrive, it's 10 p.m., but no Dhaka party gets going till late. Dinner sometimes gets served close to midnight but I know enough to have already eaten so I won't faint of hunger by the time dinner shows up. The venue is an enormous maze-like garden behind the host's mansion. Oil candles line the cobblestone footpaths, and the bushes and trees are adorned with tiny lights. There are candle-lit clearings with plush couches and silk cushions, complete with reclining couples chatting in flawless English. The DJ is playing Western dance music and the dance floor is full. The only sign that we might be in Bangladesh are the mosquito coils under every tree.

This is a different Dhaka than I'm used to. Most of my family, both from my mother's and father's sides, are middle class. Many of my paternal cousins worked their painstaking way from the village to the city. My maternal grandparents and relatives were educators and professionals, and their children have walked a similar line.

However, Tilo Aunty and her husband are both successful entrepreneurs. Their connections are far reaching and their social calendar always full. This party is squarely in the domain of the wealthy, and the wealthy of developing countries are in a class by themselves. Here are the politicians and the ministers, the entrepreneurs and the generals, the diplomats and even a strain of royalty – the descendants of the last kings of Bengal.

The open bar next to the hasna hena plant catches my attention, even though I've heard Shamayla's stories. If kids are 'doping and binging', then the adults must be too. It's just that I haven't ever seen it happen.

Tilo Aunty laughs at my expression, 'If you think this is interesting, you should check out Dhaka Club or one of the other private clubs. Some of the members have doctors' notes that say they must drink alcohol for medicinal purposes.'

'You're kidding!' I say. 'I'd love to see one of those notes. Do you have one?'

'Of course not! No woman can have one. The note basically means you're an alcoholic. Only men's reputations can withstand that sort of scandal, if at all.'

I queue up at the bar, but when it comes to my turn, I can't do it. It feels too strange, too out of place, to be drinking in Bangladesh. I feel like a child again and ask for a coke, and then four more. I dance with my vivacious aunt and uncle, but mostly, I watch. It's a sensory treat, the saris, the jewels, the tiny lights in the garden, the sumptuous food, the easy breezy conversations, even that dislocating feeling like I could be anywhere in the world.

At the edge of the dance floor, I meet Nico, wearing London stylish clothes and looking utterly at ease.

'Brilliant track, yeah?' he says winking, his Anglo accent slowed by something else.

I laugh because it's a saccharine 80's tune.

He leans in close and whispers, 'How do you think those two are getting on?' He gestures towards a couple dancing stiffly to the side. Neither looks remotely happy to be there, let alone with each other.

'You mean, *if* they are …' I say, wondering what it is he smells like. Toffee? Tea?

'Come dance then,' he says.

I shake my head, feeling even more out of place.

'Suit yourself,' he says shimmying ridiculously into the crowd.

I watch, unable to stop smiling.

After the hartaals break a few days later, Shamayla and I visit an import-export mela. The market is set up less than a mile away from the famed Parliament Building designed by Louis Khan. On the way, I make Shamayla's driver cruise around the imposing stolid structure 'floating' on a shallow lake. Visitors are no longer allowed on Sangsad Bhaban's actual premises.

More's the pity because its surrounding expanse of green is rare respite in this crowded city.

The mela boasts stall after stall of bangles, textiles, kitchenware, furniture, and leather goods, curving along a path shaped like a giant figure eight that runs through the square. I've heard that lots of people in Dhaka wear western clothes, so today, I'm wearing a long skirt and modest blouse instead of a traditional outfit. But when Shamayla picks me up, she looks bemused. Apparently non-traditional wear is acceptable around the wealthy neighbourhoods of Dhaka, not in a bustling public fair.

'Don't worry,' I tell her as we walk through the mela gates. I'm cringing at my blunder but determined to act cool. 'I won't speak English in front of anyone.'

She bursts out laughing, drawing even more looks our way. We both know that even if I could speak Noakhali, the almost incomprehensible dialect of Bangla that my father's side of the family speaks, it would still be clear that I was foreign. Not that Shamayla blends in much better. Rail thin, she's a full two inches taller than I am, and at 5'5", I'm already a giant among women. I wonder how Simi or Maher would fare here. Simi is even taller than Shamayla and her pale prettiness has always attracted attention. Maher is taller still and currently sporting a shoulder-length rockstar haircut. I'm pretty sure the three of us together would stop traffic, no pun or flattery intended.

A group of Bangladeshi policewomen pass by, the first I've seen. They are walking around in stylish uniforms: close-fitting blue saris, starched dupattas, crisp long-sleeve blouses, sunglasses, and up-swept hair.

The mela bangle stores are a wonder. Floor-to-ceiling

shelves with thousands of bangles in every colour you can paint
on: metal, glass, shell, and plastic. The sound of glass bangles
clinking together is one of my madeleines for Bangladesh,
but they won't survive a suitcase ride to the States. I settle for
the bright metal ones which are less than a dollar a dozen. A
hundred multi-coloured bangles later, I leave the store. Shamayla
doesn't blink an eye. Almost every girl in Bangladesh, rich or
poor, has a stash of jewel-coloured bangles.

After strolling through the crowds for a couple of hours,
Shamayla asks me if I'd like a drink. I nod, and we duck into
a food stall. The vendor hands me a thick glass bottle of Coke
with a straw and I am overcome with nostalgia. In Nigeria, the
only time we were allowed to drink soda was at family dinner
parties. We'd sip Coke or Fanta in between bites of spicy food,
our eyes watering from the combination. Later, the glass bottles
would be rinsed and put back in the crate to be returned to
the bottling plant for refilling. It still feels special to me to
drink Coke, despite its ubiquity in America. The glass bottle
alone clinches it.

The next time I venture to a market a few months later, I
dress as conservatively as I can, a simple yellow shalwar kameez,
a dupatta draped around my chest and wrapped about my
shoulders for good measure. Karwan Bazaar is the largest open-
air market in Dhaka and outside Tilo Aunty's office. She isn't
concerned about my taking a solo walk through it, but sends
along her assistant to trail behind me, just in case.

The market is made up of stalls crammed with CDs,
cigarettes, baskets full of live chickens, fruits of every kind, jerry
cans of water, bright bolts of cloth, yards of mosquito netting,
and much more. I want to take photographs of everything but
I manage to stop only twice. I think that at any given moment,

there are fifty people watching me, and watching so intensely that my skin is crawling.

I've been a foreigner my entire life, but I've never felt as out of place as I feel in a country where everyone looks like me. I've walked through crowds of African men, unhurried. I've danced with abandon among raver Asian kids. I've chatted easily with American housewives. Here, where it seems it should be the most natural, it isn't. I'm dressed native to a T, speaking my best Bangla, and still, a peddler cries out to me.

'Apa, ashen!' And then in English, 'Come, sister! What country you from?'

Yours, for god's sake.

The dirty concrete path through the market is bordered by a narrow gutter of slow green water, cutting into the earth. The sunlight filters through the tin roofs and blooms on a fruit stall ahead. Everything in the stall looks like it's glowing. Oranges sit in ochre pyramids. Bananas hang in voluptuous stalactites, connected by thick twine. Pineapples poke their spiky heads through the limes.

I should stop. I almost slow down as I step in front of the stall. Two little boys are huddled around a rusted metal object, staring at me open-mouthed. The peddler's voice hangs in the air with the ripening fruit. The entire scene vibrates in my vision. I walk into and out of a painting.

I see Nico on the outskirts of the market, holding a video camera, filming the crowds. This time he's dressed like his boom operator, the uniform of the urban Bangladeshi man: thin cotton button-down shirt and trousers, though I'm fairly sure his scuffed trainers cost more than a rickshawallah's annual wages. He sees me and to my distress, swings the lens in my direction. I stand there awkwardly as even more eyes train on me.

'Don't fret. I'll use that bit for my own private footage,' Nico grins at me, as we are ushered into the lobby of the Sheraton Hotel by servile staff.

We've come here for a drink, and because Nico and his team are living at the hotel while they work on a documentary film about garment workers. I'm curious how he juggles his contradictory life: high-class living, bottom-rung subjects. French-born, British-educated, Bangladeshi ancestry. But Nico is not at all conflicted. All wide eyes and earnest smiles, he uses the polite form of address for the staff and the familiar form for managers, pretending a language barrier which, while as large as mine, is only a cover for his social politics. I am so charmed by his manner, his context-conscious dress, his third grade Bangla, I even let him invite me to his room, order me a cocktail, kiss me.

When I get back home, my skin is radiating heat. I can feel it coming off my body. Eyes closed, I force myself under the shower, cold pinpoints of water shooting from the rusted metal. My breath bursts out, my skin beads up, my breathing fills the room. The water drains away noisily. It's as if I'm outside myself, watching and listening, and a girl with wet brown skin is gasping her way through a cold shower in a foreign land.

In my room, under a whirring fan, it's a sticky eighty degrees. I climb inside the mosquito net with little bloodstains all over it, mosquitoes caught fatally in the act. A tiny roach crawls atop my net ceiling. None of this fazes me anymore.

I lie on my bed and write, but all that comes out are vignettes, sensations, snapshots. The bangle stores. The fruit stall sculptures. The stiff dancing couple, with Nico making eyes behind them. The fizzy sting of cold Coke down my throat. When I try to write out these scenes, it's America narrating.

Even the rude resplendence of Bangladesh fades from all but the setting.

The light blazes through the rough cotton curtains. It's too hot to think, too hot to write, too hot to sleep. I turn on my side so I have the least amount of contact between my body and the bed, though this wafts the stale smell of my bedding closer. Gold bangles weigh down my arms and my palms are stained with mehndi, mahogany carvings along my fingers. I watch the fan flap its dusty wings above me, rippling the mosquito net with its fatalistic rhythm. *Sleep.* Enough. *Sleep.* For now. *Sleep.*

the sixth season, 31°C
I used to be sad
about not having an identity
then I thought it was liberating
not to have roots
now I am envious of you
with your nation in your voice
and I am angry
at Bangladesh, at Nigeria
for rejecting me
at America for taking all kinds

Inside History

In about ten days, Bangladesh will erupt in Language Day celebrations. Abbu has come to Dhaka to attend the festivities. His room in our Uttara home has been set up carefully. He's the first-born son, and since Dada, his father, died, he's also the de facto head of the family. Since I've grown up without an extended family, I have little context for what this means, in Nigeria or America, let alone Bangladesh. What I do see is immediate deference and meticulous attention to his needs. There are toilet paper rolls, new sheets and blankets, paper napkins, a spotless house. Forks and knives have been procured, washed, and laid out, because my father doesn't eat with his hands. He never has, despite a ubiquitous national tradition, not even when he was growing up in the village.

Abbu's widowed sister, my Hasina Fupu, lives in this house in Uttara with her children, but it is my father's house. He had it built years ago when we thought our family might move from Nigeria to Bangladesh. We moved to America instead and the house in Uttara sat empty for years, until Fupu moved in.

My first and only disagreement with Abbu takes place within a few hours of his arrival. He suggests that I make Uttara my home base. But I've been staying in Shantinagar with Nanu, my maternal grandmother, who has been very ill in recent years. Twice last year, my mother boarded a plane from Pittsburgh to Dhaka, on twenty-four hours' notice, when Nanu was diagnosed with heart failure. Miraculously, she recovered each time.

'I have to make the most of my time with her, Abbu. She was so sick last year.' Although I am trying not to sound strident, I can hear the strain in my voice.

So does my father, because he ends the thread with a non-committal shrug, 'Okay, do what you want.' And then more gently, 'How is your book coming along?'

'I have a lot of material,' I tell him, because it's the only thing I can say with certainty. I do. Everywhere I turn is another narrative, each person I meet another character. And I am taking so many photos, I have to divide each month into multiple albums.

The Liberation War Museum is my first jaunt with Abbu. It's in an old house, itself a part of history as it belonged to one of the hundreds of intellectuals who were murdered during Bangladesh's war of independence. Many of the exhibits are of clothes worn by generals and guerrillas and freedom fighters. Letters and newspaper clippings and photographs have been painstakingly photocopied, laminated, and framed on the walls. A glass case in one room showcases skulls and bones stacked indiscriminately on top of each other. It's not like

American museums with their gradual spotlights, flawless text, and haunting soundtracks. These displays are like the memories they represent, recent and raw.

You did what we could not.

The words the Igbos had said to my parents when they settled in Nigeria, three years after the Biafran War. This brutal civil war, which ravaged southeastern Nigeria and left its survivors desolate and starving, ended only two years before Bangladesh's own struggle.

Six rooms, three hallways, one stairwell in a dank old house. I have a strange pain in my stomach the whole time and I can't tell if it's indigestion or emotion. What did Bangladesh accomplish in its fight for secession, to uphold cultural identity irrespective of religious belief? What did Biafra? I don't like or understand borders, nor do I have any sense of nationalism. I am even more wary of religion. It seems they are such divisive and deadly lines in the sand. Or perhaps region and religion are just the most tangible factors. We will always find ways to hate.

Outside the museum, our driver Sohel is waiting in the shade, smoking. He's a wiry little man with an ambitious moustache and a nervous eager demeanour. He sees us, puts out his cigarette and walk-runs to the car. One of our relatives has lent us a car for the day and Abbu and I are spending most of the day in it, which is unsurprising given the traffic. Within minutes, our car is at a standstill, hemmed in by local buses, all brilliantly coloured and banged up beyond belief. I roll down the window to take a photo and my five senses are beset by every form of urban pollution.

'Roll it up! Roll it up!' my father cries out in consternation.

I roll up the window chastened, but when I look at him,

he's fashioned a bandit mask out of his handkerchief and tied it over his face.

'Well,' he says as I burst out laughing, 'I have to be prepared for your hanky panky.'

During our time together in the car, my father and I speak almost wholly in English. We do this in America too, which is one of the reasons my Bangla is piss poor, Simi's even worse and Maher's downright embarrassing. I think it's only when my family is talking about what's for dinner that Bangla comes consistently into play, which is why I don't know the English words for most of the spices I use in cooking. Otherwise, we talk about everything in English: politics, history, education, religion, law, government, science, literature. Every geography covered except that of the heart.

I cannot tell Abbu about dating Nico. We've begun seeing each other regularly since our Sheraton rendezvous. It's a confusing thing, given our tentative ties to Bangladesh, and our divergent flight patterns, though I'm willing to let it play out for now. My first love, Glenn, and I shared the same brain despite vastly different pasts and heritages. Nico and I are both a generation removed from Bangladesh, living synchronous gypsy artist lives. In some ways, it doesn't work as well. I am uncertain about a future with him, despite his endearing expectations. I had no doubt with Glenn, no matter how much we fought.

It's not just my family's dysfunction that disallows talk of dating, let alone dating itself. Asian culture is often limited to two paradigms, where you marry the one chosen for you or more recently, the one you choose, but you do either right quick. The test-drive phase is unacceptable to many families.

Given that the liberal Bangladeshi Muslim dating pool in America is fairly shallow, Simi and I have ventured wider. When

Simi chose to move in with her partner, an American scientist,
it came with a pitched battle with my parents even though
they liked him quite well. They eventually relented, seeing
their genuine commitment to each other and, we joke, the
preponderance of graduate degrees. Maher, while determined
to find his own way, is more invested in matching our family's
culture and religion. All three of us would defend one another
without qualm or question, but we'd rather talk politics than
love with our parents any day.

In the middle of our conversation, Abbu calls over to Sohel
in Bangla, 'Ey, Sohel mian!'

'Hah, sir!' Sohel replies. He's hunching over the steering
wheel as if to bodily urge the traffic jam loose.

'Your horn's voice is broken. Won't you fix it so it can sing
again?'

And Sohel and I are unable to respond because we're
cracking up.

It's taken me this long to realize that your grasp of language
changes who you are. I used to think that language was a
means of expression, a natural extension of a person. I didn't
see that personality could live apart from speech. Living in
Dhaka and my father's visit changes all that. Amma has often
alluded to Abbu's wit and humour. My siblings and I had always
shrugged her off, seeing no sign of fun ourselves. To us, Abbu
is the professor, stern, meticulous, formal. But that's in English.
In Bangla, he swings from proper to patois in the space of a
sentence and his angle never fails to surprise me. It's true that
everyone contains multitudes. I just hadn't grasped that one of
my father's was the jokester.

Not that Abbu lets go his lectures. We find out that Sohel
has two kids back home and he hasn't sent his daughter to

school despite her being of age. He soon gets an earful about the necessity of education, particularly for girls, since they have enough disadvantages without being illiterate to boot.

If I judged myself accordingly, my own linguistic performance and thus personality make it clear: in Bangla, I am a simpleton. My language skills are such that I can explain the psychological reasons I avoid eating meat, but not the political or environmental ones. I can describe Simi's love match, but I can't adequately explain why it makes sense to choose your own partner in a place where families and friends are flung thousands of miles apart and so you better damn well click with the one person you get to see every day. My gaps in vocabulary force me to dance around topics, go off on tangents in order to explain the gist, sometimes unavoidably avoid the very thing I want to talk about. Niceties of polite conversation are my first victims.

'Come to our house this Thursday for dinner,' a cousin entreats me on the phone, not knowing that I accept few invitations because one leads to a dozen more.

'I cannot come,' I say trying to convey apology with my tone since I don't know the word for sorry. I know how to say 'forgive me' but it seems a bit much.

'Then come on Friday for lunch, after Jummah prayer.'

'No, I cannot come on Friday.'

'Will you not come to our house at all?' she asks plaintively.

'No, I will not come at all,' I say, repeating her sentence structure, and then realizing how it sounds. 'I mean I cannot. I have work …'

I hope she takes my bluntness for what it is, a language barrier. It's hardest with my father's side of the family. Most of my cousins from that side of the family live in Dhaka now, but they all grew up in Barahipur, a tiny village three hours southeast of Dhaka, in the district of Feni. Their English skills are more limited than my mother's relatives, who grew up in Dhaka. When I was young and visiting Bangladesh in the summers, these disparities in our cultural, geographic, and linguistic histories didn't matter. A jump in the pond or flick of the carom piece didn't require assimilation or empathy on either side.

It is as an adult that I become a stranger to my paternal cousins, and they to me. The fact that the boys are all men now, and I a woman, makes it even harder to relate. It is with their wives that I am expected to converse, even though we've just met. Luckily, every single one of my cousins had a well matched arranged marriage (and in one case, chose wisely). My bhabis are gems, each sharper, more hysterical than the last. Give one an inch, and the mile was spent laughing, at the expense of each other and their unknowing husbands.

But I am hard pressed to answer their endless questions, in Bangla no less. After they overcome their initial shyness, they are insatiably curious. Who is it I'm holding a candle for in America? There must be someone. Who wouldn't choose to get married, after all? If I'm not at this rotten old age, I must not want to, right?

One of my sisters-in-law gets my love of the travelling life as she's the only one who's left Bangladesh's borders. But she thinks I might want to be a nomad forever, which is not the case. Another sees why I might not wish for all the responsibilities that come with starting a family. But she probably doesn't know the importance I place on commitment and loyalty.

'You're alone!' sings the dismayed chorus.

'I'm different,' is my reply, prompting laughter all around.

They're laughing because the word I used, onnorokom, also means crazy, like in a bad mental way. I know this. I'm trying to acknowledge that I'm not who they want me to be, since there isn't any hope of explaining my reservations about the legal, social, and patriarchal institution of wifedom. Not in Bangla anyway. In Bangla, I leave my listeners with the impression that I don't know what I want, and perhaps haven't even understood the matter altogether.

It might be a hopeless task to try to regain some measure of the fluency of my childhood. And now that I am aware of it, I'm more troubled with the idea that my father has spent all my life outside his country, speaking a language that appears to trap him into one limited version of himself. I wonder if he even realizes he comes off differently in English than Bangla. I wonder if he minds. Perhaps having children interacted with his language, and because he spoke English with us, it made him sterner. Or maybe having us made him more serious, made him speak English. Chicken or egg?

Inside the compound of Bangla Academy, stalls are being erected. It's the beginning of the month-long book fair and not everyone is set up. My father has a list of four books he wants to buy, but tracking down each publisher's stall appears to be a futile task. It seems there is no order to the order of the stalls. When we finally find the information booth, the extensive list of publishers they have printed out is not alphabetized. My father and I look at each other askance and then trip over each other to ask why.

'We have no software to do that,' comes the mumbled reply. Hmmm …

Despite a rapid thumb and willing manner, a search of the list produces only one publisher on the list. We collect one book and keep wandering. Luckily, the dust isn't bad. It's early afternoon, after lunch, and most people are likely enjoying a Friday siesta. By chance, we stumble across a second publisher, one that the information desk promised was *not* on the list. The man behind the stall counter looks like a baul singer. He has a deep bass voice and long hair to match.

'Now, why have you been hiding your stall from the mela organizers?' My father asks him with a straight face. Both the man and I start laughing at the idea.

'Sir, we should be on the list. We set up yesterday,' he says, his voice rumbling through his chest.

Abbu responds, 'I've walked my legs off looking for you. And I still have two books left to find. Tell me, what should I do?'

Somehow, my father manages to sound graceful through his complaint. Maybe it's his long-suffering tone, or his age that elicits tolerance. Or perhaps it's that in Bangla, Abbu comes across exactly as he intends, in this case, persuasive. The man sits Abbu down, gets his list, and sends a boy running to find the other two books.

On the 21st of February, all roads to Shahid Minar are blocked to non-pedestrian traffic. My father and I walk a mile to get to the Language Day Memorial. The path we take winds past the imposing National Museum, into the sprawling campus of Dhaka University where the students first defied the West Pakistan government.

I am learning history, not through textbooks, but through living anecdote and literature. The British-centric history I learnt in Nigeria and then in the States seemed irrelevant, disconnected from the real. But the stories I'm hearing now are palpable with feeling, tableaux come to life.

My eighty-year-old grandmother remembers visiting

America in the 1950s for a women's conference. There were separate water fountains for whites and blacks, separate eating areas. Her hosts had to get special permission for her to use the whites-only bathrooms. My mother, missing her old childhood home, sent me an email this morning about a stroll she used to take on her way to her uncle's house. She would skirt giant ponds and on their banks, she'd jump on the water hyacinth bulbs littering the path. The hollow flowers crushed under her feet with small explosive sounds. It's a vision of the city before it was laid over by concrete and high-rise buildings.

And now, here is my father, walking into his own past, taking me with him.

In the years following Partition in 1947, there were two edicts causing unrest in then East Pakistan. The first mandated that the official language of Urdu be the only publicly spoken language across East and West Pakistan, despite Bangla being the main language of East Pakistan. The second forbade people from assembling in groups of four or more, which was meant to suppress protests.

On 21 February 1952, the second edict was broken by the students. Three students were killed and scores more injured. Three years later, my father was among the protesters, in the ongoing marches against West Pakistani rulings. He was arrested and spent the next two months in jail. He was to take his Bachelor's exams from prison. In less than two decades, these uprisings and others would ignite the civil war that would culminate in revolution and independence for Bangladesh.

This is the first time my father has been in Bangladesh in the month of February, since his fateful march in 1955. As we walk towards the memorial, he recounts memory after memory.

'Here are the gates I marched through with my friends.'

'This is the wall I scaled to try and escape the police.'

'And there, my daughter, is the spot where I was arrested, fifty years ago to the day.'

The soundtrack and backdrop to his story is overwhelming. Handcuffed pickpockets are begging for release from the security guards. Impossibly crippled beggars lie on the dirt with tin cups for change. Dust-grey palm trees line the wide avenues. Crowds in beaming colours jostle past us to get to the memorial. The hawkers peddle their wares.

I didn't know they had cotton candy in Bangladesh. Hawai mitthai's literal translation from Bangla is 'sweet made of air.' The food carts are stacked with bite-sized apples, sliced cucumbers and carrots with spicy dipping sauce, star fruit, and french fries dyed red and green and neon yellow. Other vendors have little flags and tin can drums, apple-seed necklaces and bright plastic toys, balloons, and carved wooden knick-knacks.

A constant commotion issues from the loudspeakers and gatherings on every block: choruses singing national songs, poets reading, lecturers and comedians and magicians. As we get closer, we are subsumed into a solid moving mass of people. Then we're there, and the flowers fill my vision. A sea of multi-coloured marigolds covers every last inch of the ground in front of the white pillars of the memorial.

As I take photograph after photograph, a ragged little girl tries to sell me a ripe rose. I demur and then finally give her two takas, worth only pennies. I've paid too much. She returns and hands me another bloom for free.

When we return home, there's an old trunk sitting in the living room. One of my cousins found it under Dada's old bed in the village and has brought it back to the city for Abbu. It turns out to be full of books that Abbu had bought when he was young.

'I was preparing for a career in literature,' he says.

'You were?' I say astonished. Then I realize in a lightning flash why he has been so supportive of my writing. It's not just the revered place that writers hold in Bengali culture. Abbu was a writer himself.

'Yes. I even wrote a novel, in Bangla. It was published, well received even,' he says smiling. 'There used to be a copy of my novel in the National Library. Now I don't know. I don't even have it myself. It was so long ago. Before I decided to become a scientist. I have moved so many times since then.'

I trace his path in my head, from British Raj India to East Pakistan to West Pakistan to the States to Iraq to Libya to Nigeria back to America – and now in Bangladesh. Seven emigrations, four citizenships, two careers, over seventy years. My mother's path is almost as twisted. In sixty-odd years, she's emigrated five times, changed citizenships three times, borne children on three continents, and taught in two.

The books in Abbu's old trunk are legion – works by Nobel Prize winners, renowned sociologists, scientists, politicians, psychologists, philosophers, and critics.

'I had very little money, you see,' Abbu continues.

His eyes are on the edge of watery, jowls beginning to collect under his chin, more gravel in his voice. I've never been able to imagine my father young, but I can see him growing older. My mother, on the other hand, often displays a sweet glee that reveals her inner child.

'I couldn't be indiscriminate with my purchases.' He picks up a mouldering copy of *The Grapes of Wrath*. 'Each one had to be a gem. A classic.'

I turn the tattered leaves of the *Kama Sutra*, and then set it aside for myself. It feels nice to own and read my father's old books. Rousseau's *Confessions*, Zola, Camus, Maupassant, Moravia, and Steinbeck all find their way into my pile, along with poetry by Omar Khayyam, T.S. Eliot, and Zeb-un-Nissa. The prize is a 1958 first edition copy of *Doctor Zhivago*. As he sorts through the wormed tomes, he tells me about each author and how they tried to change the world. I listen, and I am a child again, in awe of my father.

A few days later, some of Abbu's old friends come to visit. He falls silent as they begin to argue about politics, religion, and government. The thread of the conversation is getting narrower and more conservative, and he can see that I'm becoming incensed. He winks to keep me still, but when one of them starts criticizing NGOs, the non-governmental organizations, even he can't resist any longer. He lights into his friends about social welfare, the power of secular and democratic governments, and compromising for the greater good.

'It's true Grameen has its problems,' Abbu agrees when Dr Muhammad Yunus's Grameen Bank microfinance project comes up. 'But let me ask you this. Have you read his book? No? Well, read his book and then we'll talk.'

Abbu also blasts the existence of a religious right that has any influence on courts of law. His voice rises in that professorial tone I remember from my childhood.

'Just as Muslims were marginalized in India, so are we marginalizing the Hindus, Buddhists, and Christians in Bangladesh. We are not learning from our own misfortunes. For example, instead of honouring only one religion's holidays, the government should ban all religious holidays!'

His old friend sputters, 'You cannot just eliminate these holidays!'

'Well then, give everyone a set number of days, say twenty days. You choose to take off whichever twenty days you wish according to your religious desires.'

This suggestion doesn't sit well with the men, but they are cowed by the force of Abbu's tone. They dare not argue even when he goes so far as to say that the electronic calls to prayer that flood the country five times a day amount to little more than noise pollution, as blasphemous as that statement might seem.

I want to applaud when he's done, even though I know his politics don't always pierce family boundaries. After Glenn, I had thought that dating Shreyas would be more palatable to my parents, because of the similarities between Bangladeshi and Indian cultures. Instead, that relationship was the centre of one of the worst fights I had with Abbu, the old Hindu–Muslim divide deeper than I can understand.

My father, with his legendary temper, even more ferocious will, lives at odds in America. Ambitious, religious, progressive, judgmental, intellectual, proud, accomplished. In Bangladesh, he is all of the same things, and somehow, as out of place.

My last outing with him is to a lychee garden near his hometown of Feni. Our guide is Nurul, a freedom fighter from the Liberation War. Mud flecks pale against his skin, his foot long healed from a gunshot wound almost four decades ago. He leads us down a furrowed dirt path to a great old battleground now host to picnickers under a tapestry of trees.

I'm not listening to his conversation with my father. I'm absorbed in the light as it drifts between bamboo and blue sky, in Nurul standing barefoot, in a checkered lungi, next to my father in polished leather shoes. It's the tail-end of winter, one of the six seasons of Bengal. They are subtler than the Western seasons, so I can only tell three of them apart, but Bangladeshis can pinpoint the arrival and departure of each. Nurul gestures in the air and my father laughs. I catch a snatch of speech.

'It's not the archangel bringing the rain because of our prayers,' Abbu is saying. 'It's the science of weather, the art of chance.'

Nurul nods, 'Clouds bang against each other.'

I imagine a celestial war, clouds like lovers, coursing in, crumbling, liquid as they meet. It makes me think of Nico who grew up on the southern French coast, obsessed with the sea and the wind.

He sometimes tells me in that way I know he's translating from French to English in his head, 'It's a rhythm I found in you.' Then switching to Bangla, a further translation, 'You are candy in my pocket.'

'I am spoiling in your pocket,' I tease him back in Bangla.

'Be mine anyway,' he says smiling.

A mud house bends the path around itself. A naked child is peeping out at us, hiding between a bright wet sari and an opaque petticoat hanging from a clothesline. I don't know how much Nurul gets each month in return for his service to Bangladesh. What I do know is that the walls of the house are smooth, freshly basted. The broom strokes on the ground outside form a hypnotic visual rhythm.

'I don't care how many times you pray,' Nurul says, his voice sliding once more into my soundtrack. 'If you murder somebody, your hands will never be clean.'

'Spoken like a freedom fighter,' Abbu says.

Nurul shrugs, 'It's only part of the truth.'

The leaves of the lychee trees judder.

'And not one part of it,' my father replies, 'comes cheap.'

When Abbu returns to the States, I find myself bereft, missing his Bangla jokes, his finicky ways. He's taken with him his encyclopaedic knowledge about Bangladesh, no matter the topic, social, political, dialectal or historical, but what strikes me most when he leaves is that he calls it going home, whether he's speaking in English or Bangla. Even though there is no doubt in his mind where he's from.

This doesn't mean he'll ever understand my triple-cum-halfway life as a Nigerian-born Bangladeshi American. Certainly not the bits about love, hapless or hopeful. What it does mean is that he forgives my linguistic lapses, whether formulatory or fundamental. Despite our essential philosophic differences, he knows that there is more to me than what I'm saying and how I say it. Personal experience has taught us both that language is elemental – describing who we are, yet telling only part of the story.

translucence, 32°C

yellow door, emerald field
fetch water from the well
fissured door, wet field
don't say the rooti fell
black burqa, white sky
the tilapia thrash in the net
burqa billowing, wide sky
there's work for you yet

Green Green Is the Ground

Despite the new smooth roads, it takes my cousin, Ehsan Bhai, and me close to five hours to drive from Dhaka to the district of Feni. The broad two-lane highway is well kept, but overused by every manner of vehicle, man, and beast. Once we enter the village of Barahipur, it's like being a planet away from Dhaka. There are hardly any roads, let alone traffic, and when night falls, the human silence deepens.

My paternal grandfather's lands have ponds full of fish, waterlogged paddies growing various varieties of rice, a chicken farm, lentil and vegetable gardens, and fruit trees galore: pears, guavas, mangoes, oranges, and bananas. His house consists of four rectangular buildings laid out in a square. A courtyard in the centre is strung with clotheslines. Painted floral designs for the last village wedding adorn the walls, floors, and steps.

I'm allotted a different bedroom each time I visit the village. This one has a yellow door, creaky window shutters, two colossal metal wardrobes, a green mosquito net, and a dressing table that has drawers filled with junk from another era.

'Your Dada died in this room, in Ehsan's arms,' Hasina Fupu tells me as we pass through my grandfather's old bedroom on the way to the dining rom.

'Oh,' I say, that simple statement making his death and his life more real than anything has before.

Because no one lives in this old house permanently anymore, it gets dirty in the way that unused houses do. Dirty in the village is a different kind of dirty. It's like in Nigeria where the outside was a continual force.

Growing up, we had a snake problem for a while, because our house was the last one on the road. Our garden became an extension of the jungle, and thus a playground for its inhabitants. After a bad scare with a snake in our pantry, my mother sewed long fat sandbags that we pushed against the cracks under every door in our house that led to the outside. It was one of my chores to make sure all the sandbags were in place for the night before going to bed.

America is so sanitized, you forget the outside's power, its filth, its relentlessness. In Barahipur, I cannot forget it for a second. In the evenings, when the insects come out in full force, I am supremely grateful to be inside my little green netted house. One night, there's an enormous beetle, an inch-and-half long, trapped and flitting wildly about my room. As I tuck the edges of my mosquito net under the mattress, every inch of the way, I am reminded of my old childhood chore with the sandbags. I wonder if the jungle still creeps into our old yard, or if more houses have been built, pushing the jungle further away.

The next day, a spider as big as my hand sits near the squat toilet while I hurriedly take a bucket shower. Outside is the constant cheeping of chicks and the quacking of ducks, overlaid by an unending hum of human conversation. The village is full of life, and there's not much privacy. Since I'm sort of a spectacle, I have to be careful when I need to change my clothes or do something else private. If I don't lock the window shutters and bolt the door, someone peeps in, usually a child who wants her picture taken.

Each day, I go on a long walk through the village. The rice paddies are such an extraordinary green, it makes me joyous just looking. Miniscule dirt roads made of dry red earth bisect the primal-coloured landscape, the palette of my childhood.

An entourage of children follows me on my walks: nieces, nephews, servant children, neighbourhood kids. They offer running commentaries without request. I'm glad because I don't have much information about this place, so I am more than happy to learn which fruits are ripe, where a snake was found among the water lilies, whose goat that used to be.

In return, I sing to them. Songs I learnt as part of the Penn Choral Society, the harmony to the soprano melody, the black key bits. Our practices were every Monday night and I almost always missed them. At the last minute, I'd drag myself away from problem sets, from love affairs, from sleep, because I knew what would come over me when I left that practice room after two hours of singing: euphoria. There was a Rachmaninov song we sang one year. Every time it got to a particular cadence, a lowering harmony, I would start crying like clockwork, singing *kyrie eleison* through the tears, my hair standing on end.

In Barahipur, it doesn't matter if I sing classical music or nursery rhymes, Christian hymns or Michael Jackson songs. It's the words the kids want. They listen to the strange sounds, spellbound, and they beg for more.

My favourite of the kids is Rekha. She's ten years old and works as a live-in cook and maid. She can't read English but always pages through the books in my room. One morning, after insisting on making my bed, she finds a photograph I'm using as a bookmark in one of my books. It's one Nico took of me the past summer in Barcelona. In it, I'm sitting on a balcony, squinting into the sunlight, drinking wine, my legs bare and crisscrossed. I like the shot because I know Nico is sitting across from me on the balcony, half-naked and lazy, snapping photos, while the Sagrada Familia rises like a dream behind him.

'You look crazy in this picture,' Rekha exclaims.

I laugh. I know few Bangladeshis, especially ones from the village, who would appreciate this photo.

'Why crazy?' I ask, curious.

'You look like a black person.'

My hair is wild and windblown and my skin darker, signs of a summer spent by the sea, but I don't look *that* much different.

'Why do I look black? Or crazy?' I ask.

'The way you are sitting. Pagol. It's crazy. Black people sit like that.'

'And how do you know this?'

'I know. I've seen them on TV.'

Little does my young friend know, I have even more reason to love this photograph if I can be mistaken for black, crazy or no.

Hasina Fupu comes into my room with a pile of sunwarmed clothes. She's the youngest of my father's siblings and my father has always paid special attention to her, especially after she was widowed with five children. In turn, she dotes on Abbu in her abrupt matter-of-fact manner.

'My mother, your Dadi, didn't speak the last months of her life,' she tells me.

The planes of her face are smooth and flat, the darkening age spots a familiar map. She straightens her shawl in her no-nonsense way and opens the almari.

'She just lay there, her eyes closed. We would turn her, clean her, feed her, but she seemed to sleep through it all.' Hasina Fupu's eyes are far away. I can tell she is watching Dadi as she sleeps.

'She who ran our house with a steel will. Everyone always knew where she was, whether she raised her voice or not.'

The hawker outside falls silent, swallowed into the hush of midday heat.

'And now you could almost forget that she was in the room.' Fupu's lips twist as she speaks. It might have looked like disinterest or bitterness, if I didn't know her better.

'It was years after she died that I learnt the word coma.' Her tone is wondering.

The English word, coma, is distorted. I don't even recognize it at first. Then it settles into the memory, lies down with Dadi. Hasina Fupu closes the almari door. I can see her in the mirror as she leaves the room, her feet turning out ever so slightly as she walks.

'It must have been that,' she says to herself. 'A coma.'

When Rekha invites me to her house in the village, I accept. Her family's home has five rooms, not including the separate kitchen and stand-alone bathroom. It's made of a combination of tin and thatching. The house is filled with aunts, uncles, grandparents, cousins, brothers, sisters, in-laws, and babies. I am brought a chair from another house and seated, as if on a throne. Unbeknownst to me, in honour of my visit, Rekha's father has bought a fortune's worth of cake and biscuits and cold drinks. This is especially a waste, since my Nigerian prejudice against sweets still holds.

No one has any trouble understanding my primary school Dhaka Bangla, but I can't decipher the Noakhali dialect, so I keep asking Rekha to translate. Rekha's mother is a sharp and dominating woman with lips stained purple from the paan she chews.

'Where is Kasim Bhai?' Her teeth, blackened nubs protruding unevenly along her gums, stump me even more than her question.

'Who?' I ask, when I recover.

'Kasim Bhai. Your father.'

'Oh, Abbu. He's gone back to America.' I keep forgetting about the numerous names and nicknames Bangladeshis have, including my father's.

'Where's Boro Amma? She didn't come this time?'

I haven't heard this term before, but I guess that she's asking about my mother. 'No, Amma had to stay in America. She's teaching –'

'How is Maher?' she interrupts.

'He's doing well.'

'What is he doing?'

'He graduated from university and is working, in business.'

I wait for questions about Simi or me, but after it's determined that neither of us are married, nothing more. Simi and I have five graduate degrees between us, but only the male heir's career prospects are important. I happily let myself be dragged off by Rekha who wants me to photograph the family goat.

The next morning, I am awoken by my nieces banging on the door.

'Come Fupi! They're calling you!'

I climb out of the moshari, wrap a dupatta around myself and unbolt my door. They lead me to the front pond where half a dozen men are raising a net filled with fish. Although the pond isn't clean enough for bathing anymore, it's still rife with tilapia. The fish are brought into the front courtyard and Ehsan Bhai directs the division of the catch. The fish are thrown flopping into piles and, once divvied, they are collected in buckets by villagers and taken away.

A lovely girl wearing a blue and white shalwar kameez is standing across from me, watching the fray and me. She smiles shyly, pulls her dupatta close around her shoulders and edges closer to speak. Nipu is sixteen, bright and entertaining and warm. Her little two-room house is within my grandfather's compound and has obsolete calendars flapping on the walls as some curious decoration. When she offers to show me the sights of Feni town, a short rickshaw ride away, I accept with enthusiasm.

After a delicious fried fish lunch cooked by Fupu, I meet Nipu outside her house and am disconcerted to see her svelte figure swaddled in a burqa. She's even wearing a matching black gauze veil. According to her, this is standard fare for any teenage girl in Feni venturing outside, if they are ever allowed, that is.

'But I don't have a burqa,' I tell her, leaving out the fact that I wouldn't wear one in any case.

'It's fine, because you're from abroad. But I could never go out to town otherwise. My mother wouldn't hear of it. Only when I was much younger, when I wore dresses, then it was okay.'

As we trundle to town by rickshaw, every woman I see is dressed in head-to-toe black and most often veiled. Nipu says it has always been this way, but when I visited Feni in the early 90s with my mother, I don't remember it that way. Nipu was a child then. It makes me sad to think that my grandmother and her generation fought so hard for women's rights, for the abolishment of the purdah, and with some success too, because my mother and her friends did not grow up wearing headscarves, let alone burqas. Now it seems Nanu's work, in that domain at least, may have been for naught.

Feni Town boasts massive ponds, the likes of which no longer exist in Dhaka. Our rickshaw circles around one and then drops us off at a coconut garden. We wander through it and end up in a shady mango orchard, the branches so low above us as to feel like a leafy tunnel.

Closer to town, Nipu finds a park chockfull of flowers and we settle down for a chat. As we swing on a swing-set, she tells me about her dream to go to Dhaka University once she's finished with high school.

'But my parents won't pay for my last year of school,' she tells me. 'They think they have already paid too much and it will hurt my chances of marriage.'

'Do you think it will?'

'I don't think so. And besides, I want to be able to take care of my family. What if my husband doesn't do his part? My cousin has this problem and she can't even clothe her children properly. I have a part-time job in Feni Town and I'm learning so much. I want to have my own way of making money. Then, whether or not I get married, I can take care of myself and my family. But I need to finish school and go to university.'

Despite her earnest tone, her direct gaze, I have no idea if Nipu needs money for what she's saying. In a country this poor, there is no end to the heart-breaking stories. Local or foreign, people have different strategies for dealing with solicitation. Some people don't give alms. Others keep small change handy in a separate purse. Others donate through charities and NGOs. It's unclear to me which option is best so I do any of the three, depending on the occasion and my state of mind.

With Nipu though, it doesn't matter. Any girl who can tell me a story like that after growing up here is worthy. I don't care what she wants the money for. I give her everything I have on me and borrow more from Hasina Fupu when I get back.

'What can I give you in return?' Nipu asks me. 'I have nothing. I can only pray to God to give you blessings.'

I don't want prayers but am too afraid to say so in a place as god-conscious as the village. Anyway, what if God were some version of magic, or some superlative apprehension of beauty, or simply the feeling of awe? Might joy itself be a reason to believe?

'You can do one thing for me,' I say.

'Anything.'

'You said you know how to use the Internet, no? Get an email address. Write to me. Tell me how you're doing every so often,' I smile. 'Keep it simple because I don't read Bangla that well.'

My last night in Barahipur, I go for a walk on my own. Tomorrow, I return to Nico, to my book of stories and photographs, to the mad megacity that Dhaka is. I'm surprised to realize it feels like going home, though I know I will be taking the village with me in some form.

Everyone in my grandfather's compound is glued to the TV watching a natok, but I can't stand the overdramatic acting that characterizes Bangladeshi stage theatre, so I slip out. It's cloudy out and I can see the moon only occasionally. I come to an open space where the rice paddies reach the horizon on both sides of the narrow dirt road. Since I can't see much, I close my eyes so I might hear better. A million frogs croak in the waterlogged paddies. Ducks and wild dogs cry in the distance and the crickets are ubiquitous. Down the road, a rice mill hums.

When I open my eyes, there are fireflies everywhere, moving constellations in the translucence. The night is perfect: cloudy, moonlit, immersed in underlying light and sound.

What I don't realize as I walk content back to the house is that my disappearance has caused pandemonium. At least twenty people are outside scouring the area for me. I have been gone less than fifteen minutes, but it is long enough to raise an alarm. No one, especially a woman, goes walking at night alone.

'Is it dangerous?' I ask.

'No, no. It's just not done,' Ehsan Bhai tells me. 'But what would have happened if you had fallen in the darkness?'

'Or gotten lost,' Fupu adds.

'Or been kidnapped?' A more hysterical neighbour chimes in.

'Weren't you frightened?' Rekha whispers, tugging at my dupatta.

'No,' I say. 'I only wanted to take a walk and I'm very sorry for all your worry.'

To make it worse, my parents have happened to call from America to check up on me, perhaps raising the first alarm. Abbu is in a grand state of shock upon hearing that I can't be found, in his old village home to boot. Ehsan Bhai hands me his mobile phone. I apologize again, even more contritely and tell him and Amma about the rice fields and the cloudy moonlight and the frogs and the fireflies.

My extended family hears the last bit about the fireflies and a joke evolves about how I went walking to see the jonaki. I hear them laughing, but I don't protest. Fireflies are a good enough reason for me.

cloudburst, 33°F

here I love you
in the neon-streaked night, your streets rise and roar
the hoarse hawkers and blighted beggars
vie with their ululations
a hundred times I listen
horns, whistles, engines, breath
a thousand times I hear anew
oh the lurid flutter of your clothes
beckoning
the sultry hoods of your rickshaws unfurl and wink
saris weep and wave from your crumbling balconies
this is a window
here I love you

Writing Home

The rains have begun in Bangladesh, that same force of nature I remember from Nigeria. When I moved to America as a teenager, I found the temperate spring season weak, spitting water from an emasculated sky. Two decades later, I am once again living with tropical rain. The kind that comes with gunshot thunder, eye candy lightning. The kind that falls so hard, so fast, you cannot separate the air from the water.

This is my second monsoon in Bangladesh, and my first Kurbani Eid. Babu Mama, the uncle who taught me to swim when I was a child, has bought a massive black cow, which is waiting outside Nanu's apartment building in New Eskaton. It sits idly, decorated with red and pink ribbons, swishing flies with its tail. Other goats and cows are tied up nearby. Meanwhile, a crowd is gathering behind a large camel being led down the street by its proud owner.

In the days before Kurbani Eid, numerous open-air markets selling cows and goats spring up. Nanu says there will be blood everywhere on the day of Eid, that if it falls in the summer, the stench of flesh and blood could drive you out of the city, maybe even out of the religion. Many people leave the city and go to the villages for Eid, but poor villagers often come to the city to beg for meat. For many, it's the only time of the year when they are able to eat meat. They dry what they procure in the sun, half-rotting by the road sides. If it doesn't rain soon after, the smell will linger for days.

Years ago, I dated a vegetarian who didn't like the idea of using the same pots and utensils for vegetarian and non-vegetarian food. It proved too hard to keep everything separate, so I stopped cooking meat at home and then stopped eating it as much. This habit hardened when I moved to the Bay Area, where vegetarianism was more common and the produce and restaurant options were better than on the East Coast, not to mention the strong food politics against eating meat. I still avoid meat as much as possible, though I do eat fish occasionally. My Bangladeshi taste buds might be too strong to give that up just yet.

But it's more than the mass-slaughtering and eating of animals that makes me averse to Kurbani Eid. The holiday is based on an old story, written in the holy books of all three monotheistic religions. In it, God asks Abraham to sacrifice his child to prove his faith. And Abraham does, or at least tries, and for centuries after, Muslims around the world have celebrated this disturbing call and response. But I want to be a good sport so I peel myself away from my writing to get ready.

As per Eid tradition, I wear new clothes. Nanu has bought me a red and orange shalwar kameez. The bright colours remind me of the dresses that my uncle brought to Nigeria when Simi and I were young, of the fight that first showed me that I was righteous, too sure of my memories.

My cousins emerge, showered and resplendent in silk kurtas. We go downstairs and take photos of our cow. The parking lot of our building has been cleared of cars. Each family's parking spot is its sacrifice area. Butchers have been brought in, and the lot is filled with bleats and moos. I don't want to watch this part, so I go back upstairs.

Mrs Hussain, who lives next door to Nanu, comes to wish our family Eid Mubarak. She's worked up as she's gotten off the phone with her son who lives in America. They've had their usual fight about marriage. Her son is willing to get married but he'd like to meet the girl and get to know her before saying yes or no, but neither Mrs Hussain nor the girls' families think this is necessary. One or two conversations or 'dates' within a week should be more than enough.

'A week!' I exclaim.

Even though so much of the conversation about me in Bangladesh has centred around my unmarried state, I haven't been de-sensitized to the issue. Sometimes I start to think everyone's right, until I remember the fact that I have never seen as many unhappy marriages as in Dhaka. Marital misery and with it, divorce rates, are rocketing, though this appears to give no one pause. It feels like an epidemic to me, not just the divorces, but the marriages themselves, but I can't say so out loud.

It's a divisive point with Nico who has wanted to marry me from the beginning.

'It's as if you aren't listening, as if you don't care,' he had complained, the last time he had brought it up.

'I am and I do, but I don't see how you can be serious,' I had told him gently. 'You proposed that first afternoon at the Sheraton. The first time we kissed!'

'And I meant it then.'

I hadn't known what to say then and still don't now. Premature protestations or not, it's unfair to point out his timing. My uncertainty has nothing to do with that. Not that I know what it has to do with.

'Listen, my dear,' Mrs Hussain says, snapping me out of my tangent. 'A week is being generous. Not all of the families will even give this much. His next visit to Bangladesh is not until next month and these girls, they cannot wait that long. They want to know his decision because they have other offers. And I cannot tell them anything because he refuses to commit without more *conversations*.'

She says this word, conversations, with some distrust, as if it's not sane, certainly not proper, to want this thing.

'All he keeps saying is he wants a girl with a good personality. Personality!' She pauses and looks up for sympathy, then continues, 'Where am I going to find a girl like that? A good family, nice-looking, modest behaviour, what else can you ask for? Personality? When I was to be married, my uncle poked my back and I said what I should and that was all the personality needed for the match.'

Nanu is smiling. She has said nothing so far. She's waiting for my protest and I oblige.

'But you can't expect someone who doesn't believe in arranged marriages to accept this. There are generation gaps and cultural differences you must consider.'

Mrs Hussain sighs, 'I know, I know. I am not unsympathetic. But things don't work that way in Bangladesh. He must get married and soon.'

My cousin, Raaef, interrupts our conversation as he bursts into the room, 'Come and see. It's done!'

'Oh no, you got blood on your kurta!' I say pointing to a prominent stain on the white silk.

'Oh, it's fine,' he says. 'Lucky even, to get a spot like that on your Kurbani Eid clothes.'

I wrinkle my nose and follow him out of the flat. The elevator is packed with people carrying plastic bowls filled with chunks of raw meat. A man lifts a large leg of a cow, hoof and all, and carries it out of the elevator. I realize that its bloody haunch had been leaning against the elevator wall, the same wall I'm leaning against now. I jerk away from the wall.

'I promise I will never touch the sides of this elevator again,' I whisper to myself.

'What's that?' asks Raaef, grinning.

'Nothing,' I say, though he's probably guessed at my squeamishness.

The parking lot is running in blood. I step over the streams gingerly and head to our parking spot. Our cow is unrecognizable, but its various parts are pointed out to me, as they hang from rope, dripping blood, like a horror movie clothesline.

When I go back upstairs, I pace outside the flat. It's cool on the landing and there are spectacular if hazy views of the city. The man who had brought up the cow leg in the elevator carries it out of Mrs Hussain's flat.

There's a maid close on his heels and she's yelling, 'Why didn't you cut it up before bringing it to us? You think we eat hooves here?' She hands him a cleaver, 'Make sure you cut it off before bringing it back in.'

He sighs and props the cow leg up on an empty paint can. The hoof seems to watch us both in reproach. He attempts to saw it off and I am unable to stop watching. Finally he gives up and takes the leg back into the elevator.

One week before Victory Day on 16 December, the military is deployed in Bangladesh. Four out of ten cabinet members resign in protest. The traffic blockades and hartaals are at an end, but the coming January elections remain in doubt.

In terrible tandem, Nigeria also suffers failed elections with vote rigging, violence, ballot theft, and intimidation. I watch on the Internet as bombs and armed clashes strike all over the country. This, the country that boasted the most promise around the time I was born, that had survived the Biafran War, and one corrupt dictator after another, emerging each time only to fall back again into chaos. Our family had left in the late 80s, thinking things were bad then. Little did we know how much worse it would get. I wonder what Nsukka looks like now, if these trials and others have worn down its bright intellectual pride. Despite everything, I still want to go back.

With Bangladeshi politics, the more I read, the less I understand. Each thread of research leads to three more that confuse me even more. I peruse the papers, listen to my Dhaka relatives in one party, my non-resident Bangladeshi parents in another, and everyone in between. None of it helps.

The people who make the most sense are the maids and drivers who work for my relatives. Tuhin is the driver for my cousin Shamayla's family. He has a gruff schoolmaster's way about him and stands at attention when I'm in his presence. It's expensive to live in the city. Tuhin's flat costs a majority of his wages. Then there's the English-medium schooling that kids can't do without these days. No matter that Tuhin never learnt English, but his older son must. The younger one is only three, and naughty, so Tuhin is going to put him into a madrasa, following an old tradition in which one would save a child for God.

I've never met him but I picture Tuhin's younger son. Perhaps he has his father's curly hair, but not cropped so close. Perhaps he climbs everything in sight and shouts out each conquest. Perhaps he's the way I was when I was three. Family legend has it that my first word was 'neejay', which, in Bangla, means, I'll do it on my own. Except at age three, in addition to my Arabic surahs, I was learning Bangla, English, and Igbo, and my own curly-haired father had every ambition that I would grow up to advance the field of knowledge, to have a hand in changing the world.

After I crawl under my mosquito net each night, I lie very still and the words wane out of my mind. I think about the feelings I'm trying to capture in my writing and photography: Rekha's forthrightness, Tuhin's resignation, my sense of futility. I had thought it would be so novel to write about characters set half a world away. My stories are about maids and madams, village kids and VIPs, artists and addicts, in Bangladesh. But it turns out, people agonize about the same things no matter who they are, where they live, or how much they know better. It's all about love, money, family.

My ideas about volunteering have also been up ended. I've always liked helping people, especially women, see things differently, singling out and supporting their powers. But in Bangladesh, I'm the one being shown the power of women. Last year, I volunteered at an NGO that focused on women's rights. The office was filled with women hard at work educating others, teaching them their rights, giving them options. This year, I'm working with a small labour rights organization that helps garment workers and undocumented labourers. The woman who runs it is a former child worker herself and she astonishes me daily with her charisma and compassion and hard-won self-taught philosophy.

It's humbling to realize how much braver these women are than me, not only the helpers, but the ones being helped. Often, they're the poorest, the most oppressed, but somehow they come to understand that they might deserve more. They have the gall, the glory, to ask for it. Would I have done the same if I hadn't been encouraged every step of the way? I'm almost sure not. I am in awe. Filled with it. Surrounded by it. Giving it away.

Nico's activist film projects in Dhaka have transitioned into progressive TV journalism and his tenure keeps being extended, his assignments alternately dangerous and dull. I have no sense of urgency, even though our time together is filled with laughter and light. It's as if we're still sitting on that balcony in Barcelona, together yet separate, the dream of love hovering in the background.

My time alone is even more joyous. I am overcome with every rain-wet leaf, every wide-eyed gaze, every flashing bangle, never-ending fodder for my collection which is finally starting to look like a book.

When I do see people, it's mostly at family events. Siraj Bhaiya is the eldest of my paternal cousins and his home in Mirpur is a natural gathering spot as his sister's family lives in the same building. His flat is on the fifth floor and the bedroom balcony has lovely views of the city. The living room balcony is on the opposite side of the flat and overlooks a lake nearby. Like every other major and minor body of water in Dhaka, this lake is banked by ever-expanding bostis, slums, which increase the city's mega-population by a factor of two or more. The makeshift one-room shacks push to the edge of the lake and sometimes end up perched on stilts above the water. The homes are constructed along rows which are a metre wide, just enough room for a person or two, to walk between.

I've stood on Siraj Bhaiya's balcony for hours peering down five stories to the narrow paths between bamboo walls and tin roofs. Some of the slum inhabitants have split off electrical lines from the streets and fed the wires to their houses to power TVs and refrigerators. Today, I am watching a rickshawallah fixing his rickshaw outside his house, talking to his wife, who stands at the door. Numerous half-clothed and naked children dot the road, playing varied games. Two little girls who have been ousted from a recent game are wearing bright rags of dresses and running after each other, their lank hair browning in the sun.

Siraj Bhaiya comes out and asks me why I'm taking photographs of the bosti.

Without looking away from my camera, I answer, 'It's another part of life, Bhaiya, isn't it?'

'It is. They have their own lives down there. They give birth, they celebrate, they grieve, they die. What will you do with your pictures?'

'I'll write about them,' I say as the shutter clicks.

'Now we have two writers in our family,' he says proudly. 'You and Jetha, your father.'

I smile. One girl has stopped to look at a twisting kite. The other follows her pointing finger to the sky.

'But what you see is not pretty,' he continues, 'Will you write the good stories too, then?'

I nod though I'm unsure of my abilities, even with the ready tragic. I am jealous of Nico and his motion pictures. What little I capture with my words and photographs are two dimensions of many. He gets to record sound and motion as well. The lilt of a lover's sigh, the tilt of her chin. Not that any of this, not my nor Nico's art, even comes close to the reality of being in Bangladesh. The colours alone fell me. Cerulean water barrels, a lime-green kameez with a hot-pink shawl, blood-coloured mosquito nets. The most threadbare cotton sari is a technicolour dream. The beauty will not stop if you want it to.

Despite the anachronism, the decay, everything moves. No matter that a machine looks 100 years old, or that a painstaking process is entirely human-powered. It's not always forward motion nor fluid, but everything is in a constant state of change.

I now recognize each of my myriad nieces and nephews by the shrill of their voices, hear stories from my grandparents' time, and listen to my aunts and uncles talk about what it was like to grow up in the subcontinent, post-Partition. It's not my history, but the force of family love, the respiring city, is absorbing me into itself.

Even as this web tightens, I can tell I will leave. Dhaka has become another home. But this place I ostensibly come from is far from Simi and Maher and my parents, who are, in the end, my first home. They came before America. They came even before Nigeria, before the dust-blown sun-lit town of my childhood. I'll go back to them, to the family that knew me before I knew myself, just as I'll come back to Dhaka.

'There is always something missing,' I tell Nico in one of our final conversations. We've decided, or perhaps I've decided, that our resonances aren't enough to sustain our relationship. We're breaking up and it's proving more painful than I thought, as if I didn't get it until I walked away.

'And there is always something found,' he replies.

My father says that in order to be a writer, I have to know a place, which, to him, means living somewhere for a long time. He's since retired from geology and consulting and has returned, with startling prolificity, to his first career, to literature. His fiction is set in Bangladesh, a country he has not lived in over half a century. It's written in Bangla, a language he doesn't speak on a regular basis, a language he no longer dreams in. Yet somehow, this is indisputably home territory.

What he doesn't know is that it might be too late for me. It might always have been. I might never know a place so deeply to come back to it half a century later and write two novels and three story collections in the space of five years. The ways I will never measure up to my father abound. What I'm hoping for is a lesson that comes from the surface of things, poised in stop-gap motion, real in transition. I might be able to create something from the so-called skim, from the outside in.

The leather box shaped like a teardrop is empty now. Its carmine lining will never hold anything but the smell of what couldn't be. The memory of my fall is as vivid as ever, but I'm no longer on dangerous earth. Or if I keep repeating this, it will become true, the same way I made myself up and made it stick.

For now, I revel in the now. It's only tomorrow that I'll think twice. It's only the past that drags me down. It's just me in this slow exquisite present, not waiting for the morning, with its grace and its grief.

bow echo, 73°F

10.04 p.m.

It's bed time. Wendy comes in and straps her wrists loosely to the narrow metal frame. After fastening the ties, she looks at her. She tries to focus back but can't, so she closes her eyes. She hears a whisper, 'You'll be all right …'

She opens her eyes, but there's no one in the room. Have her eyes been closed for minutes or much longer? It seems less dim, less dangerous.

> My whole day I was racing against darkness. I don't think I even knew it. And once I was alone, I crumpled.

She used to love the nights, but they are too long now. The mornings bring relief, an end to the darkness that consumes her so wholly that she expects never to find her way back again.

> I think I mistake
> my exultation for grief
> my lust for apathy
> I think I don't realize
> that I have too much in my heart
> not too little

Limbs outstretched, she watches the sky suffuse with light, and thinks of a Russian folk tale from a childhood book. In the story, a poor child, Vasilissa, is plagued by an evil witch to perform impossible tasks. If she doesn't finish them by morning, the witch will eat her. Each night, she is saved by a little doll that her mother had given her before she died. The doll tells her to go to sleep, and morning will come with its fortune, because, 'Dear Vasilissa, the morning is wiser than the evening.' And of course, Vasilissa awakes each morning to find the impossible done.

> I'm losing faith
> in losing faith
> it never leaves me

Epilogue

apparent horizon, 93°F

at the end of Odim Street
she marks the late afternoon
with her walk, like clockwork
when the sky strikes ash blue
past the tender alamanda flowers
the rocket hibiscus
the thorn tree towers
if you wait for her here
she'll walk you
through the waking
of the evening

Wiser than Evening

The women outside the car are shouting, each one with a brightly-coloured jug at her feet, a small cup in hand. The bush is close to the road here. I can smell the green, the jungle trees. I am thinking of nothing, just breathing.

'Try this palm wine.'

'Try this one.'

'No, *this* one!'

Nearby, a massive garbage heap rises metres high, hosting two dozen grazing goats. At the very top, two billy goats with horns rear at each other, one full on aggro on his hind legs, forelegs high in the air. The sun turns the whole scene into a silhouette, darkening the rubbish into a three-peaked mountain. The sewage swamp surrounding becomes a shallow lake and the goats are armies at the ready, their kings already at war.

When the man in the back of our taxi finally decides which jug of palm wine he wants, we drive on. An hour later, we arrive at Lokoja, at the confluence of the massive Niger and Benue rivers. The taxi driver made the same trip the day before and boasted of driving his car through knee-deep water. We are hoping he was exaggerating.

In fact, in the twenty-four hours since, the Niger has risen and Lokoja is underwater. Riverside houses are almost totally submerged, with only their top-floor windows showing like desperate eyes. The road ahead of us has vanished, children body-surfing the surface of the flood in glee. The rest of the Lokoja residents sit on the verandas of the houses, just barely out of reach of the water, and watch in silence, mattresses and other narrowly-saved items piled nearby.

'This thing. Can you imagine?' says the driver.

'Honestly,' replies the woman passenger in the back.

We abandon the flooded road and follow the line of cars leading into the bush. The path is hilly, unpaved, and unmarked, beset by treacherous ditches and puddles, and barely wide enough for cars. There is an equally eager procession of vehicles coming from the other direction and it takes us an hour to get back to the road.

Soon the road goes underwater again, but luckily, only tire high. We drive through it slowly and reach dry land, only to come to a stop inside the most monstrous traffic jam I have ever seen. Miles upon miles of trucks, buses, and cars, in total standstill, in boiling heat. Worse than anything I've ever seen in Dhaka.

No movement is possible, not even to give up and go back. Every inch of road and pavement is taken up. Even the motorcycles are hard pressed to zip between the lines for more than a few metres at a time. Three blazing hours pass, children crying in the heat and people leaving their transports and climbing up the construction site to the west to pray, or walk the edges of the hills back home, or god knows what.

Our driver is young, impatient, hot-headed. Against our better judgment, he somehow scrapes and muscles our car to the other side of a line of impassive trucks, some even facing each other, head to impossible head.

We end up on the flooded 'sidewalk' next to the yawning river. Our car inches along until we come to the head of the monster: a hundred metres of road under waist-deep water. The driver switches off the engine. We gather our belongings on our laps and we watch as the Niger takes over the world.

When I was a child, the University of Nigeria Nsukka was surrounded by walls. There was only one entrance to UNN. It was at the top of a hill, barricaded by a gate and guards. Now, nothing looks familiar. There's a long processional corridor with sweeping lamp posts. Flat land. I'm baffled. I have had a map of the campus in my head for as long as I can remember. I have walked it in my daydreams for the last twenty-five years. How could I forget the very entrance?

As we pass the university hospital and come onto Fulton Street, I realize where we are. We have entered from the opposite side of campus. It's only then that the driver the UNN has assigned to me, Fidelis, says the back entrance is new, bypassing the bustle of the outer town of Nsukka.

When the vice-chancellor of UNN heard I was coming to visit Nsukka after decades away, it didn't matter that he had no idea who I was, nor that he had never met my father who taught Geology for fourteen years at the university. Or even that I am only coming for one fleeting day, en route to America, a

small financial windfall and an even smaller window of time,
making the trip a reality. Charmed by my story of homecoming,
he arranges for Fidelis to pick me up at Enugu Airport and
drive me to Nsukka.

It's noon when we arrive. It's just rained and the ground
is a shining red. The flame of the forest trees are dripping
with flowers and water. My first request is to stop at my old
primary school. The vast assembly grounds and back playing
fields shrink in my adult eyes. The concrete bungalows of
classrooms are more compact than I remember, and the tree by
the headmistress's office is not nearly as massive. The secondary
school classrooms have been taken over by the kindergarten
classes and the new secondary school is in a different location
altogether. But the broken or missing window panes of the
buildings are the same.

The actuality of Nsukka is both staggering and shabby,
reduced yet redolent. This thing I have dreamed about for so
long is finally happening. It is so unexpected a gift, so strange
and yet so ordinary that it feels anticlimactic. I am a ghost,
wandering an invisible place, behind a scrim of a flesh-and-
blood stage. My overriding sense is one of forlorn relief.

I find the classroom where in grade 6B, I memorized 'The
Tyger' by William Blake, a poem I can still recite by heart. And
I visit form 2X where I learnt to draw the human skeleton
from scratch and got whipped by the French teacher for every
botched utterance. When she hears of my visit, the headmistress
calls me into her office.

'You have come back home!' she says. Her smile is enormous
and encompassing. 'You are welcome.'

As I have long suspected, there is no one left here I know.
On Facebook the night before, I find a classmate from Mr Eze's

grade 6 class. He is now a banker in Imo State and his name is familiar, though I don't recognize him from his picture. I ask him about our classmates, the names coming to my tongue slowly, satisfying. Obiageli, Liam, Nnamdi, Onyeabo. The onyochas, the foreigners, have gone to America, India, England. The others have moved to Enugu, Lagos, bigger cities in the south.

When I ask about my old friend, Nneka, he hesitates and then tells me a terrible story. Nneka's mother died when Nneka was a teenager. She entered medical school with bright prospects, but her sanity was already in question. Her first year was scattered, unstable, and by her second year, she was wearing the same dirty dress for days, her eyes far away. She died soon after, perhaps committing suicide, though no one knows the whole story.

This story reverberates in my head as I drive through Nsukka. I lost touch with Nneka within a year of leaving Nigeria, my letters going unanswered or lost. For years, I imagined us living parallel lives. We'd finish high school, go to college and graduate school, get married, have kids. But it seems our parallels crashed, perhaps even around the same time. I returned on a great circle, to a pendulum world, melancholy and ecstatic in turn, alive. But with Nneka's mother gone, her father distant, her siblings and friends unable to reach her, she never came back.

As it gets to later afternoon, while navigating badly deteriorated roads, I find what I think is the very first house my family lived in, on Odim Street. It's easier to find our second house, on Ako Okweli Street, a corner plot at the end of the road, at the edge of town. The jungle used to sit, whispering, on the other side of our hedge. Now there is an apartment building there, pushing the green farther away.

The compound is smaller. Part of it must have been cut off because there isn't enough space for the second garage, which is no longer there, nor the mango trees Simi and I used to climb when we were children. The front garden is wild and overgrown – not a hint of my mother's precisely laid out patterns of rose and allamanda bushes, cactus plants, and frangipani trees – but it is lovely in its own wild right.

I beg permission from the current residents of our old house and begin an old ritual. I stand at the very southwest corner of our compound, now shaded by a brambling tree. I push the leaves away from my face and I turn to the setting sun. I was thirteen when we were about to leave Nigeria and I could sense a terrible impending loss. So I stood in that corner every evening for a year before we left and I memorized the crawling hills, the coiling jungle, the violent sky.

So much has happened since then that I don't know what to think, or even, what to wish for. So I just stand there on the red wet earth in squinting sunlight and I thank everything and everyone that has brought me here, that has resulted in the incarnation that I am now, that I will be in another quarter century, if the accident will.

Then I get back into the car and I leave Nsukka in its golden hour.

Acknowledgements

- Excerpt from Kaiser Haq's 'Two Monsoon Poems', *Published in the Streets of Dhaka: Collected Poems*, UPL Dhaka, 2007.

- Excerpt from Cecily Parks's 'Beast-Lover Variations', *Field Folly Snow: Poems* (The VQR Poetry Series), University of Georgia Press, 2008.

- Excerpt from Uche Nduka's 'Whereas'.

Thank you to the editors of the publications in which these excerpts appeared previously, sometimes in different forms.

- The 'bow echo' vignettes were performed as a one-act play at *APAture*, Fall 2002, and were published as one piece under the title 'Wiser than Evening' in *Switchback*, Fall 2004.

- 'Tyger Tyger' was published under the title 'Ironed Blue Sky' in *ZYZZYVA*, Fall 2004 and anthologized in *Literature, the Human Experience*, 9th edition, R. Abcarian and M. Klotz, editors, St. Martin's Press, August 2005. It was also a finalist and was published in the *Aesthetica Creative Writing Annual 2012*.

- 'Dhaka at Dusk' was published under the title 'The

Satisfaction of Tears' in the *Aurora Review*, Winter/Spring 2005, and reprinted in the *Daily Star*, 7 January 2006. The poem in 'Dhaka at Dusk' was published in the *Pittsburgh Post Gazette*, 24 July 2004.

- An excerpt from 'On Growing' was published under the title 'One Two Three' in the *Daily Star*, 10 September 2005, and another excerpt won the *Wasifiri* New Writing Prize 2011 for Life Writing. A 600-word excerpt was selected as a highly commended winner in the 2009 Commonwealth Short Story Prize.

- 'Chameleon Girl' was published in the *Daily Star*, 12 November 2005.

- An excerpt of 'Inside History' was published under the title 'Father Tongue' in the *Daily Star*, 25 February 2006.

- 'Judo Lessons' was published in *Swink*, December 2008.

- 'Green Green Is the Ground' was published in *Terrain.org*, The Migration Issue, May 2012.

- An excerpt of 'Enter the Living World' was published in *580 Split*, Issue 14: A Gathering of Voices, June 2012.

- 'Standing in the Sun' was published in *Bengal Lights*, Spring 2013.

- 'Beatrice' was published in *Your Impossible Voice*, Issue 1, Fall 2013.

- 'Hieroglyphics' was published in *Wasafiri*'s Special Issue on Writing from Bangladesh (#84), November 2015.

★

Olive Witch was my first completed manuscript. It's perhaps my favourite because the past is an impossible place to visit, and my childhood has felt particularly lost to everything but my memory. This book has gone through so many iterations and has been under so many guiding lights, it may be impossible to thank everyone who had a hand in its making. Many of the following are in the book and others were generous thoughtful readers.

To my mother, whose tenderness belies the adventure. To my father, nomad professor, his own peregrinations showing me that the world is wide. Both my parents honour writing as a noble profession and that made it all the easier to begin. To my sister Simi, whose story this is because we grew up so close in age and adoration. To my brother Maher, third culture kid, who somehow fits in everywhere. To the Ullahs: Nana (pbuh), Nanu, Kismet Mama, Snigdha Khala, Shopna Khala, and Nasr Mama, who drove 1000 kilometres to Nsukka to be there when I was born, and who have been with me since. And to Nanu, my maternal grandmother, for my first taste of feminism of the highest order.

To U, my best friend in Nsukka, generous and brilliant girl, you are remembered. And to Matu, whose letters were my link to Nigeria after I left.

To Eshadee, honorary Hoque sister, for teaching me how to dance. To Kelly, for those afternoons on Fifth Avenue. To Todd, for sitting beside me in the Elizabeth Forward High School cafeteria day after day and eventually getting me to speak. To

Arshad, for giving me my first camera seventeen years into our friendship (I still love that swivel lens). And to Miss Ditter, for not cutting me from the high school swim team.

To Glenn, my same brain first love, for all the things we learnt together over seven years. And to your parents, Ann and Roger, who have kept me close to this day. To Sheba, who I never have to explain anything to, except the obvious. To my favourite JimChae, for solace and always making me laugh. To Tom, for your pop song whimsy and wisecracks. To my Wharton advisors, Jerry and Steve, for believing in me, no matter how hard I made it look. To Goose, for the Epsom salts. To Dave Toc, my first and favourite boy watching companion. To Rahim, for not having cab fare after Woody's. To Bonny, for your fierce and funny friendship. To Chris and Teresa, who helped me stop counting match castles. To Natalie, for knowing when to leave, something I still haven't learnt. To Arati, for looking after my pew. To Stokes, who knew to head west before any of us. To Cynthia, for that night at Fluid which changed everything. To Ritu and Val, for the full moon letters. To Irene, for the romantic consults. To Rebecca, who I always imagine in motion. To Marko, for knowing what it's like to be thirteen and in America for the first time. To Bleem, British Kentuckian travelling fool, I'm vicarious with you. To Amanda W, for singing blood and fire at the castle. And to Paul, for saying it would happen.

To Ram, for the epiphany that led me to writing and for your confidence in my career. To Arif, for the poems that bind our lives. To Hardik, for knowing how to break it down. And to Amudha, for the laughter.

To Aaron, who made my poetic dreams come true by admitting me to MFA school. To Dean, most vibrant adventurer and writer, for all the rides across the Bay. To Mary, who teaches me something good every time I see her. To Jules, dark-hearted owl lover. To Cheryl, for sharing Christmas with me. To Kim-Pye, for that welcome dash of colour our first day of writing school. To Adrienne, for your careful and compassionate readings. To Bee, of the gorgeous gypsy heart. And to Stephen, best advisor ever at the University of San Francisco, who ushered the first version of *Olive Witch* into being, back in 2003.

To Alan, my perfect and perfectly curious confidante across the years and continents. To Mahmud, my tandem Bay Area and Bangladesh traveller and scribe. To Nellie, for knowing all the right words. To Camalo, for your cracked earth voice and spirit. To Suna, my braver alter ego. To Sara, for all the dye jobs and cocktails and seven course meals. To Neela, for your inspiring self and salons. To Laura F, for your wit and winsome. And to Pamela, for making me jump into the river in Loire.

To Neeta, my beloved curlygirl. To Nadiya who opened her jhaal muri loving heart and house to me. To Farah, my dance partner from Dhaka to London to New York. To Sabrina Aunty, for remembering everything except the day of the week. To Razzak, for your deep dark support, and the MRI. To Maeve, for coming to Abby's to dance. To Jogu Uncle, for the bus ride and stories all the way to Calcutta. To Zafar, for telling me to get to work. To Baby, Miron, July, and Altaf, whose stories stay with me. To Nicolas, for candy in your pocket. And to my extended family: Sabbir, Babu Mama, Nibras, Shiraji Bhai, Majib Chacha,

Hasina Fupu, Sara, Mary, Roxanne Bhabi, Ashraf, Jamie Mama, Momota Bhabi, Buneka, Ehsan Bhai, Sadia, Rifi Mami, Nani, Dottie Bhabi, Raaef, Mala Mami, Naki, Laboni, Renu Chachi, Mayaz (to name only a few, sorry!) for taking me in with so little context and so much love.

To ZYZZYVA, for my first ever publication from *Olive Witch* in 2004. To the San Francisco Foundation, for my first writing prize in nonfiction, and joyous affirmation. To the Fulbright Foundation for gifting me a year in South Asia, fodder for my first book, *The Lovers and the Leavers*, as well as the last third of *Olive Witch*. To the National Endowment for the Arts, for the literature fellowship that helped me move to New York, not so starving artist. To the New York Foundation for the Arts, for the nonfiction grant that lent me financial breathing room and an artistic community. And to Somak, my editor at HarperCollins India – my first two books exist and with more clarity because of you.

To Sharlene, from Russia, with love and crazy stories. To Durba, who implicitly understands. To Jen, for the charm and chardonnay. To Amanda D, for getting lost with me in the woods. To Laura P, for holding the door of the plane. To Andrea, for the magical afternoons. To Jamie, for always being there and having an opinion. To Radhika, for the kisses. To Laura G, for your elegant enthusiasm. And to Josh, my funny irreverent talented love, this wouldn't be nearly as much fun or beautiful without you.